"Jim Burns is a great man. In this new, wonderful book, he maps out all the outside influences that can weaken a student's integrity. I highly suggest this book for any parent, grandparent, teacher, and youth leader so they can help build integrity in today's students."

Stephen Arterburn, bestselling author
and founder of *New Life Live!*

"In *A Student's Guide to Sexual Integrity*, Dr. Burns speaks from a wealth of experience and writes in a clear and compelling fashion. He tackles the toughest issues with both sensitivity and wisdom. I will be recommending this book for a long time."

Sean McDowell, PhD, professor at Biola University,
YouTuber, and author of many books,
including *Chasing Love*

"Every teen in America is a victim of sexualization, and it is one of the biggest contributors to depression, anxiety, broken relationships, and more. Jim Burns's *A Student's Guide to Sexual Integrity* gives kids concrete ways to resist this cultural phenomenon and fight back. As a pediatrician with over thirty years of experience, I can tell you that teens want adults to talk about this and help them! That's exactly what this book accomplishes."

Meg Meeker, MD, bestselling author
of *Strong Fathers, Strong Daughters*

A STUDENT'S GUIDE TO SEXUAL INTEGRITY

A STUDENT'S GUIDE TO SEXUAL INTEGRITY

GOD'S PLAN FOR SEX AND YOUR BODY

with Erin Mashaw

JIM BURNS

BETHANYHOUSE

a division of Baker Publishing Group
Minneapolis, Minnesota

Published by Bethany House Publishers
Minneapolis, Minnesota
BethanyHouse.com

Bethany House Publishers is a division of
Baker Publishing Group, Grand Rapids, Michigan

Printed in the United States of America

Library of Congress Cataloging-in-Publication Data
Names: Burns, Jim, author. | Mashaw, Erin, author.
Title: A student's guide to sexual integrity : God's plan for sex and your body / Jim
    Burns with Erin Mashaw.
Other titles: Purity code
Description: Minneapolis, Minnesota : Bethany House, a division of Baker Publish-
    ing Group, [2024] | Reprint of: The purity code, 2008. | Includes bibliographical
    references.
Identifiers: LCCN 2024002312 | ISBN 9780764243080 (paperback) | ISBN
    9780764243295 (casebound) | ISBN 9781493446711 (ebook)
Subjects: LCSH: Sex—Religious aspects—Christianity—Juvenile literature. | Sex
    instruction for children.
Classification: LCC BT708 .B8825 2024 | DDC 241/.664—dc23/eng/20240321
LC record available at https://lccn.loc.gov/2024002312

Cover Design: Micah Kandros Design
Author Image: Scott Roberts/ Marc Roberts Photography

Baker Publishing Group publications use paper produced from sustainable forestry practices and postconsumer waste whenever possible.

24 25 26 27 28 29 30   7 6 5 4 3 2 1

CONTENTS

NOTE TO PARENTS AND STUDENT MINISTRY LEADERS

My guess is that the student in your life didn't purchase this book—you did. Frankly, I don't know a lot of kids who think, "I'd like to read a book on sexual integrity." At this stage of their life, the idea of living a life of healthy sexuality may be more important to you than it is to them. I get it. THANK YOU for caring enough for your students to help them deal with one of the most important issues of their life. When I was a student ministry leader, I used to say to students all the time, "The decisions you make today will affect you for the rest of your life." I'm not sure they totally understood that concept, but the parents and adults in their life sure did.

Just recently, I was speaking on the topic of *Teaching Your Children Healthy Sexuality* in North Carolina at one of the many seminars that HomeWord provides for churches. I began the seminar by asking the 450 parents in the audience, "How many of you received good, positive, healthy, values-centered sex education from your parents when you were growing up?" Four people raised their hands. That was it. Then I came right back at them with this statement: "Research tells us that the more positive, healthy, values-centered sex education students receive from their parents or a caring adult, the less promiscuous and *confused* they will be." Sometimes when I make that statement there is an audible groan. And, while it may be true that most of us didn't receive proper sexual education from our parents, one of our top priorities should be providing it for our children.

Here are four things I can tell you about teaching your children a healthy view of sexuality:

1. *It will no doubt be awkward.* I write and speak on this subject all the time, and my kids still tease me about those conversations being awkward. It just comes with the territory.

2. *Dialogue is better than monologue.* Someone once said, "I would rather have 100 one-minute conversations about sexuality than 1 one-hundred-minute conversation." Teaching healthy sexuality is a process. The one-time talk doesn't work. And these conversations have to go both ways. While a monologue suggests that one person does all the speaking, a dialogue involves speaking AND listening. And listening is the language of love.

3. *This generation is different than any previous generation.* They're learning to view tolerance as a form of loving, which means that sometimes they can misunderstand a historical, biblical view of sexuality as unloving to others. So, show them you can love deeply

and not necessarily agree with the prevailing culture. Be kind. Be compassionate.

4. *Try to be the safest adult they can come to with questions.* This may be a major shift from the relationship you had with your parents. Your kids won't view you as safe if they don't feel heard and loved, even if you disagree with them. The safest adult in a student's life is often the one who will have the most influence when it comes to the conversation of sexuality.

5. *Be patient.* Good, healthy sex education is a process. There will be ups and downs in this journey, but I promise it's worth it. Hang in there.

6. *Pray for your kids and this generation.* To be perfectly honest, even though I've spent my entire adult life speaking and writing on this subject, I thought I was done writing to kids. But my heart and mind wouldn't leave me alone as I prayed for this generation of young people. They are facing challenges with their sexuality that no generation has faced before.

So, let's partner together and create a fresh, new, healthy narrative on God's view of sexuality. Let's do it with love and understanding. Let's show kindness and never sway from the fact that God created us in His image.

I love this quote by Madeleine L'Engle. I have tried to live by this in my life and ministry, but especially as I wrote this book. "We do not draw people to Christ by loudly discrediting what they believe, by telling them how wrong they are and how right we are, but by showing them a light that is so lovely that they want with all their hearts to know the source of it."[1]

And by the way, at HomeWord, we continue to be hard at work creating resources to help you navigate the challenges of parenting today. We've prepared an incredible curriculum for students on this very topic. It was designed to be used in student ministry groups as well as at home with parents. We're excited about the opportunity to come alongside you as you coach your kids on one of the most important subjects on the planet. You can find this course at www.HomeWord .com.

Jim Burns, PhD
President, HomeWord
HomeWord.com

MEET THE AUTHORS

Hi, I'm Jim . . .

I've spent my entire adult life trying to help students make healthy decisions about life. At our family Christmas parties, I always sit at the kids' table. It's a lot more fun. My parents always said, "When are you going to get a real job and act like an adult?" But I've always loved being where the action is, and that's hanging out with students. It's fun, it's messy, and there is seldom a dull moment.

I'm married to Cathy. We met the first day of college and became "just friends." Okay, I hoped for more, but she immediately got a boyfriend. Because of our friendship, she would ask me what I thought about her boyfriend. I'd always give her the same advice: "Break up with that scum, there is someone better for you!" She finally broke up with him, and we started dating. I married her one week after college graduation. Most of the time I believe I'm the most fortunate man alive because she is an amazing and awesome person. One time I was introduced on TV as an "expert on sex," and she burst out laughing. Not cool, but I still like her.

We have three daughters, Christy, Becca, and Heidi. I came from a family with all brothers, but I really like being a "girl dad." They taught me a lot about emotions and drama (eye roll). We had fun going to dad/daughter dances. Those were a lot more fun than the fear of teaching them all to drive a car. I worried about them when they were students, and they are still constantly on my mind, even though now they're all married. I love their husbands, but many of my greatest joys come from being a grandpa to four of the most awesome kids in the universe, James, Charlotte, Huxley, and Bodhi. When each of my grandkids were born, part of my heart got wrapped around their hearts, and I've never ever been the same. When my daughters were students and it was time to have conversations about sex and their bodies, they said it was AWKWARD. More about that later.

The most defining moment for me (besides being born but I don't remember anything about that) was at age sixteen when I became a Christian. I wasn't raised going to church, but I started following a girl I liked to her church. I loved it. Then one night in my bedroom, I asked Jesus Christ to come into my life. I didn't know much about faith, but that one decision changed the trajectory of my life and family forever. You'll see when you read this book that I am unashamedly Christian and yet, I hope you won't find me "preachy" or "lecturey." (*Lecturey* isn't a real word but I'm sure you get it, and sometimes I like to make up words. I know, kinda weird. There I go again with a made-up word. *Kinda* isn't in the dictionary, but we all use it.) Also, as you read this book, I want you to know I will do my best to give you a perspective on sexual integrity from God's Word, the Bible. Personally, I think God gets a raw deal when it comes to what people think He says about sexuality. He isn't some kind of grinch, trying to steal all our fun. He actually *created* sexuality. It was His idea! So, I think that since God created our sexuality, we should hear what He has to say about it. And spoiler alert, you might just be surprised!

Meet Erin Mashaw

I might be biased, but I think Erin is one of the finest writers and thinkers on sexual integrity I have ever met. I met Erin when I was asked to do a series of videos on sexuality for her church, North Point Community Church in Alpharetta, Georgia. They asked me to send in the script for the filming. The day before I was to fly from California to Atlanta, I got the script back with all kinds of edits and changes. I'm not a big deal, but no one had ever changed my scripts before. Because it was the day before I was going to fly to Atlanta, I wasn't super happy. I sent a note to the guy who was in charge, saying I'd look at the changes but couldn't guarantee I'd use them. I was a bit more negative to my administrative assistant. It wasn't until later that night that I read the changes. EVERY CHANGE WAS A GOOD ONE. They made my script much better.

I immediately wrote to the guy in charge of the filming and told him I LOVED the changes and wanted to meet the editor. It was Erin. The next day she was a part of the filming, along with her sixteen-year-old son, who had to watch me speak for hours about sexuality in the studio. Awkward! Erin made some additional changes during the filming, and they were all awesome. I made a mental note that day. "If I ever write another book for students about sexuality, I want Erin to help me." So that's why her name is on this book.

15

She helped me with wording, language, and content. As a woman, she gave me the female perspective. She really knows what she's doing. Plus, she has impressive credentials. She is the parent engagement director at North Point Community Church. She has been involved in children's ministry, student ministry, and family ministry for over twenty years. She is a wonderful writer but most importantly, a great wife and mom. She is married to Reece (cool dude with a ministry degree) and has four amazing kids, Gavin, Kate, Luke, and Wyatt.

Since we're going to be talking with you about some very personal issues, I thought it might be helpful for you to get to know us. We aren't academics, even though we have some higher education degrees. We're just adults who love students and want to help you think about some of life's most important decisions. We don't claim to have all the answers to life. But we'll do our best to help you think about and develop a plan for the kind of life you really want—a life that honors the Creator who made you and loved you before you were even born. And a life that gives you the best chance to flourish.

Okay, let's get started.

Oh, and by the way, this subject is so important to me that if you have questions or need help, I always suggest you talk with your parents or a trusted leader in your church. But just in case you need additional help, please email me at info@homeword.com. While I can't guarantee that I will get back to you immediately, I always do my best to respond to every email.

Jim Burns
Dana Point, California

DEDICATION AND THANKS

Dedication

Cathy

Your love and commitment to help students make wise decisions has never wavered. If anything, you are more passionate today than ever before. Thank you for your partnership in life, ministry, parenting, and grandparenting. You da best!

Thank You:

Rod Emery, Randy Bramel, Terry Hartshorn, and Tom Purcell

Twenty-one years ago, I was so deeply fortunate to join our amazing weekly small group. I am a better husband, father, and Christ-follower because of all of you. I'm so grateful for your leadership and mentorship in my life.

Doug Fields

Who would have thought that an 8th grade kid in my youth group would become one of this generation's key leaders in the field of youth ministry? One of the deep joys of my life is watching God use your amazing giftedness. I am so thankful for your partnership in ministry and friendship.

Cindy Ward
Thank you, Cindy, for the twenty years of partnership in ministry. Thank you for reading the manuscript and making great comments. Thank you for your leadership at Home-Word and representing me so well.

Erin Mashaw
Wow! Your addition to this narrative was amazing. Your comments made this a much better and more effective book. Thank you for reading this manuscript twice and thank God for your giftedness.

Todd Dean, Tom Purcell, Bob Howard, Tracy Kuntz, Rod Emery, Randy Bramel, David Lane, Ken Verheyen, Theresa Sinclair, Ned Brines, Pat Daniels, Doug Fields
HomeWord has the best board in the world. Thank you for your support, encouragement, wisdom, and leadership. "Where there is no counsel a people fall, but in the multitude of counselors there is safety." (Proverbs 11:14 NKJV)

Greg Johnson
There is not a better literary agent in the world. Thank you, Greg.

Carol Zinngrabe
Your generosity and passion for helping students is nothing short of inspirational. Thank you so much for all you have done over the years to make a difference.

Andy McGuire and Bethany Lenderink
Such great editors. You made this book so much better.

ONE

AWKWARD!

AWKWARD! I know this subject is awkward, I get it. I've spent my entire adult life talking with students and their parents about sexual integrity. Yet, my own daughter Christy once said, "My dad has spoken to millions of people about sex and never looked nervous, but when it came to speaking to me, he was sooo awkward. His bald head would sweat, his ears would turn red, and he stuttered a lot." Gotta love the truth from your own children.

Yep! Talking about sex is awkward. It's probably awkward for you. And I know it's awkward for your parents and almost everyone else. But these conversations have to happen if we want a healthy view of sexuality. We can't put it off any longer. I'm guessing that you didn't personally buy this book. Probably a parent bought it for you, or maybe you got it from your church. But somebody in your life thinks it's time you had "the talk." So, let me say from the beginning, even though some things may be awkward or even embarrassing, what you believe and what you do about your sexual

19

integrity will be among the most important decisions of your life. It might be difficult to understand that today, but ask any adult and they'll tell you the decisions they made as a student about their sexuality played a significant role in their life. Some of those decisions were good, and some weren't. But regardless, their belief and behavior when it comes to sexuality became a major part of their life and identity.

Speaking of awkward, let me tell you about my first kiss with Cathy. I mentioned in the beginning that Cathy and I met in college. It was the very first day at freshman orientation. I was sitting in the back of the room, in the "nerd section," while Cathy was in the second row in the "cool kid" section. I couldn't keep my eyes off her. I finally told my new friends, "See that girl down there? I'm going to take her out on a date." They looked at her, looked at me, and immediately started laughing. They said something like, "Yeah, right!" The very next day we were in the same English class. I introduced myself. Later I found out she had a boyfriend, so we became "just friends." Okay, so this is where it gets awkward. My mother had given me a pillowcase with a picture of Big Bird[1] on it for me to take to college. Not cool, Mom! Big Bird was a popular character with . . . wait for it . . . preschoolers! That's bad enough, but it gets worse. Every night before I would go to sleep, I would place my lips on Big Bird's lips, pretending that I was kissing Cathy's lips. Weird. And embarrassing, right? But that's how much I liked her and couldn't stop thinking about her!

Finally, Cathy broke up with the tall, dark, and handsome guy she had been dating, and a few months later I held her hand at a basketball game. That might not seem like a big deal to you, but it was a huge deal for me. That night at a

Christmas party, I just sensed that what I had been practicing on the Big Bird pillow was finally going to happen with Cathy. After the party we went for a walk. It was the perfect night; the full moon and stars were shining. The way I remember it, birds were singing, and bells were ringing. Now was the time. I closed my eyes, tilted my head, and leaned in to place my lips on her lips but something very strange was touching my lips. I opened my eyes, and my lips were planted on her right nostril! I MISSED her lips entirely.

Talk about an awkward kiss. As I was driving back to my dorm, I just kept yelling at myself, "You missed her lips, you fool!" I walked into my dorm room where a bunch of guys were playing poker. I lay on my bed and made a general announcement to my friends, "I missed her lips!" They laughed and someone said, "Whose lips?" I said, "Cathy's lips." He said, "You will never go out with her again!" Well thankfully, he was wrong. We got married one week after college graduation.

Here's the point. You've probably heard the word *sin* before in the Bible. Some people might give a complicated definition of the word, but it simply means to miss the mark. There are a lot of people in the world who are missing the mark when it comes to their sexuality. Just like me, I was going for the lips, and instead I kissed a nostril. I missed the mark. That was embarrassing but not a game changer. Every day we get all kinds of mixed messages about sexuality. It seems like there are voices shouting at us from every direction. And listening to some of those voices can lead us to make decisions about our sexuality that can miss the mark if we aren't careful. Sooner or later, you'll need to choose which voice to trust and to follow.

Here are four things that can influence students to make unhealthy sexual decisions:

- Peer pressure
- Emotional involvement that exceeds their maturity level
- Lack of healthy, positive, Christian sex education
- Negative self-image

Peer Pressure

Peer pressure, or the pressure to conform to be like everyone else, can cause us to compromise our values. The "everybody's doing it" or "everybody's thinking it" mentality can get us in trouble. It can be easy to believe that everyone around you is thinking about, talking about, and having sexual experiences. And you might even feel like you're missing out. Don't believe the lie! Students today often brag and talk big about things they've never even done. And many times, the students who *have* done those things actually wish they hadn't. They might pretend to be proud of their choices, when deep down they're hurting and heartbroken because of the damage those experiences have done to their hearts and minds.

You might be feeling pressured by a boyfriend, girlfriend, or even just a friend to try things you know aren't wise or good for you. You can say no! Anyone who genuinely cares for you will respect your decision. If not, it might be time to put some distance in those relationships and choose to spend time with people who share your values.

Peer pressure is real. This week I talked to two students who felt incredible pressure to change their pronouns because their "friends" were pressuring them, and they were afraid of being rejected. I get it. We all want to be included and accepted. But real friends love and accept you for who you are.

Emotional involvement that exceeds their maturity level

I know that's a mouthful of words, and some of them may be unfamiliar to you. So let me explain. Sometimes you can get so close to someone emotionally that your heart can start to convince you that you're ready to share more of your body with that person. Because time and/or feelings equal intimacy. This is what I tell students all the time. The feelings you feel are real, but they can't always be trusted to lead you in the right direction. Following your heart, or trusting your feelings, can lead you to make a life-changing decision at an early age that you are likely to regret.

The more time you spend talking, hanging out, or even texting with someone, the more emotionally connected you feel to them. Your relationship becomes emotionally intimate. But that emotional intimacy can be very misleading. Emotional intimacy can make you think you are ready for physical and sexual intimacy long before you actually are.

Ashley was fourteen years old. She was totally "in love" with Benji. He was not a bad guy, but his hormones were raging at sixteen. She compromised her values and had sex with him because her emotional involvement with Benji exceeded her maturity level and she didn't have what it took to say no. The relationship ended quickly, and Ashley felt deeply depressed and used.

Many experts say that our hearts, minds, and bodies are not mature enough for physical intimacy in the teenage years.

And that's not your fault. It's true for all of us. You might be very mature for your age, but that's different from the maturity level you'll have when you're ready for marriage.

Lack of healthy, positive, Christian sex education

Most students don't receive very much positive, values-centered sex education at home. If you *can* talk to your parents about sex, you're lucky—not many kids can. Some parents aren't confident in teaching about sex or knowing how to bring it up. Your sexuality is more than what you do with your body. Sexuality involves your feelings and attitudes about yourself, as well as how you feel and act toward others.

If your parents bought you this book and they're willing to talk about sex and sexuality, be thankful! I don't know them, but I already know they love you and want the absolute best for you! And that makes them pretty great parents. But just know that these conversations will be awkward, even with the very best parents.

Unfortunately, most schools that offer family-life or sex-education programs provide what I call "value-neutral education." In other words, they talk about things like birth control, sexual techniques, and gender issues, but they don't offer any values or moral perspective. I know the schools want to help, but it's important to look at sex education through a moral and biblical point of view as well. I guess that's why you are reading this book.

At your age, it's completely normal and healthy for you to have lots of questions. It's important to ask those questions in the right place. You might be tempted to ask your friends or use the Internet to find the answers you're looking for. But there are a couple of problems with that plan:

- Your friends don't know as much as they think they do. They're trying to figure out the same things you are. For an important topic like this, you need to talk to an adult you trust.
- The Internet doesn't care about you. Your parents, grandparents, aunts, uncles, and small group leaders do. Looking online will give you all kinds of "answers," but you'll quickly find that they say lots of different things because ANYONE can put information online. They don't have to be an expert or even know what they're talking about. Even more concerning, the Internet will quickly direct you to all kinds of things (pictures, videos, etc.) that will hurt rather than help you.

So here is the question I have for you: Who is the safest adult you could talk with and trust about your sexuality? How about your parents or grandparents? Maybe a youth leader at church? Questions about our sexuality can be awkward, but having an older, wiser person to talk with is worth it, and I think you will be glad you found that person. So, before we go any further, stop and name the person that could be that resource for you.

Negative self-image

Another factor is what a person thinks or feels about himself or herself. Most of the time when I meet someone who is making unhealthy sexual decisions, they're struggling with a poor self-image. Here's part of a letter I received from a student in Florida:

> *I'm not a bad person. I'm not the best-looking person in the world, but I'm not the worst. I have an okay personality. For the last two years I've had sex with five different guys. I don't know why I always let them have their way, but I do. I guess I want them to like me, and I'm afraid if I don't let them try things [sexually], then they won't want me as a girlfriend.*

This breaks my heart! This girl wants to be liked, but she is not making good decisions. She has a very low image of herself and doesn't have a healthy view of her sexuality. There's a better way to live, and her negative self-image got in the way of it. She's not a bad person. But she made some bad decisions, and now she's dealing with shame about it. Thankfully, she doesn't have to feel shame. Instead, she can lean into God's forgiveness and grace. We'll talk more about it in the next chapter, but when she truly understands that she was created in God's image and is loved by God with an unconditional love, there will be no room for shame and no room to keep living the way she has been living.

I guess everyone can agree that talking about sex is awkward. However, it's also one of the most important parts of our life. I am totally honored that you're reading this book and truly wanting the very best for your life. So, let's move on to looking at what is so amazing about our sexuality.

DISCUSSION STARTERS ➤

Think about your answers to the questions below and talk about them with an adult you trust.

1. Jim described having conversations about sexuality as awkward, especially with parents. Do you agree or disagree with him, and why?

2. Peer pressure or the pressure to conform can be difficult for anyone. What are healthy ways to fight against negative peer pressure? Where can you find positive peer influence?

3. Many students make poor choices about their sexuality because they didn't receive healthy, positive, Christian sex education. In what ways do you think that kind of information could help students make good decisions? Who would be "safe" adults for you to talk to about things like this?

4. How do you think students your age are influenced by emotional involvement that exceeds their maturity level or having a low self-image?

TWO

AMAZING!

If you thought the first chapter was awkward, then I hope you'll think this chapter is amazing. I want to be super clear, right up front. There is absolutely nothing you could ever *see* or *say, do* or even *think* that would make God love you any less. Because of what Jesus did when He died on the cross, when your Father in heaven looks at you, He sees you as His beloved child. As followers of Jesus, we want to live a life of sexual integrity and honor God with our heart, soul, and mind. But we don't do that because we're trying to earn God's love and acceptance. We honor God as a grateful *response* to the love and acceptance He has *already given* to us.

So, as you start on this journey, there are a few things I'd like you to know. First, believe it or not, the decisions you make today can affect you for the rest of your life. And this chapter will challenge you to make important, life-changing decisions.

Sexual integrity is not just about sex. It is about living in a way that can bring you the most freedom and set your future up for joy. People who live with sexual integrity carry the least amount of spiritual and emotional baggage (bad memories, regrets, etc.) into relationships. And who doesn't want that? Here are four principles I hope you'll consider living by when it comes to your sexuality.

1. Always Lead with Love

   It's the way of Jesus. When you read about Jesus in the Bible, He consistently showed love—even to people He disagreed with . . . and especially sinners. He didn't agree with a prostitute or her lifestyle, but He still showed her love, honor, and dignity. There is no room for Jesus-followers to mock or make fun of anyone in any way. When I hear about Christians bullying people who have a different perspective on sexuality, it makes me really sad. That's not the way of Jesus. Again, you can disagree with someone and still show them love. It's what Jesus told us to do: "'This is my command: Love each other'" (John 15:17 NLT).

   Let's pretend you have a friend who is sexually active, and you disagree with their choices. Lead with love. Let's pretend that you have a friend who is struggling with thinking they might be gay, or trans, or nonbinary, and you disagree with their lifestyle. Lead with love. Let's say that you have a friend who has been looking at pornography. Lead with love. Here is what the Bible says:

   > If I could speak all the languages of earth and of angels, but didn't love others, I would only be a noisy gong or a clanging cymbal. If I had the gift of prophecy, and if I understood all of God's

secret plans and possessed all knowledge, and if I
had such faith that I could move mountains, but
didn't love others, I would be nothing. If I gave
everything I have to the poor and even sacrificed
my body, I could boast about it; but if I didn't love
others, I would have gained nothing.

1 Corinthians 13:1–3 NLT

It really can't be clearer, can it? Everything we do
is just a bunch of noise if we don't show love. The
Bible goes on to say in what is often called the "love
chapter:"

Love is patient and kind. Love is not jealous or
boastful or proud or rude. It does not demand its
own way. It is not irritable, and it keeps no record
of being wronged. It does not rejoice about injus-
tice but rejoices whenever the truth wins out. Love
never gives up, never loses faith, is always hopeful,
and endures through every circumstance.

1 Corinthians 13:4–7 NLT

Okay, just take a moment and reread those verses.
Yep, it doesn't say only love the people we agree with.
It just challenges us to love. In fact, the Bible teaches
us that love is the most important thing we can do.
This is how 1 Corinthians 13 ends: "Three things will
last forever—faith, hope, and love—*and the greatest
of these is love*" (1 Corinthians 13:13 NLT, emphasis
added).

Jesus showed love to people He didn't agree
with. Jesus shared truth with people who had different opinions, but continued to lead with love.

31

His love is amazing! And He can help us to love that way, too!

2. Remember That Kindness Matters

You are living in one of the most divided times in history. Spend ten minutes on social media or watching the news and you'll see a lot of hate, judgment, and meanness. God's ways are so different than our culture. Kindness is showing respect even when someone doesn't deserve respect. Kindness is being generous to someone who lives differently than us. Kindness matters in all relationships. Kindness changes everything. Kindness melts relational walls.

Here is what the Bible tells us to do and be when it comes to kindness: "Be *kind* and compassionate to one another, forgiving each other, just as in Christ God forgave you" (Ephesians 4:32, emphasis added).

In other words, because God offers His forgiveness to us, we should forgive others. But more than that, we are called to show kindness and compassion wherever we go and to everyone. Our family knows a guy named George (not his real name) who lives a different sexual lifestyle than what we believe in. And he uses a lot of drugs. George has problems, but he is still a good guy. Even though we wouldn't agree on some major core values, we found out that at forty years old, he hadn't had a birthday party since he was nine. So, we decided to have a birthday party for him. Cathy made his favorite meal, cheese enchiladas, and since it was a surprise, we greeted him at the door with party hats and sang "Happy Birthday." He was blown away. After dinner we brought out a cake with forty candles and sang again. In the middle of the song, he turned to me and patted my arm and said, "I thought you were Christians." I answered, "We are Christians." He looked confused. Later he told me he had never known Christians who were kind to him. You don't have to change your belief to show kindness. "Love is patient, love is *kind* . . ." (1 Corinthians 13:4, emphasis added).

When you lead with love, you are always going to be kind. Kindness is part of the biblical definition of *love*. There will be people who aren't kind to you. Be kind anyway. Because part of kindness is offering forgiveness and grace. "But the fruit of the Spirt is love, joy, peace, forbearance, *kindness*, goodness, faithfulness, gentleness, and self-control" (Galatians 5:22–23, emphasis added).

As Christians, the Holy Spirit of God lives in us, so there is no room for anything but kindness toward others. People who are mean and judgmental aren't usually happy people. They are certainly not living with the strength given to us by God's Holy Spirit. Sometimes (especially if you disagree with someone) you'll need to make a conscious decision to proactively "clothe yourself with compassion, *kindness*, humility, gentleness and patience" just as it says in Colossians 3:12 (emphasis added). If you are mean to people who view life differently than you, do you really think it's going to be helpful? Do you think it will help them to change their mind? I don't. Living out our Christian life can be a challenge. Someone once said to me, "What we say matters, but what we do matters more."

3. Live Like You're Created in the Image of God

This idea has a huge influence on how we do life and how we approach our sexual identity and integrity. In the very first chapter of the Bible, it tells us: "So God created human beings in his own image. In the image of God he created them; male and female he created them" (Genesis 1:27 NLT).

Do you believe that God created you and that you were created in God's own image? If so, there are a lot of things that will make sense for you about your life and your sexuality, as well as finding your purpose in life. I've concluded that God is my creator, and I trust that He's a lot smarter than me. So that means I need to allow God and His Word to be the authority in my life. Choosing to submit to God and surrender to His plan for you is the safest place you could ever be.

Yuval Noah Harari authored a book that even after eight years on Amazon.com is one of the most read and bestselling in the world. The book is called *Sapiens: A Brief History of Humankind.* My guess is you've never heard of Yuval or his book. It's not a book most students read. I don't agree with his premise of the book because he doesn't believe in God. Here is a direct quote from his book, "As far as we can tell, from a purely scientific viewpoint, human life has absolutely no meaning. Humans are the outcome of blind evolutionary processes that operate without goal or purpose."[1]

That statement is one of the saddest commentaries on life I've ever read. But when it comes to what we believe about our purpose, there are really only two options. Either we were created by a loving and all-powerful God, or life has no meaning or purpose at all. I'll be honest—I think it takes more faith to believe that you and I are an "outcome of blind evolutionary processes" than to believe we were created by a loving Master Designer, God.

God created us. And it just makes sense to me that whoever designed you gets to define you. God created every part of you with a plan and a purpose. In the creation account of the Bible after God created man and woman, He saw it was "very good" (Genesis 1:31). This means that God is the creator of our gender and sexuality. He created sex to be good. God can be trusted to want the best for us. And that's pretty amazing, isn't it? If we believe this, then we can trust Him as our designer, creator, and the expert on our worth and value.

4. Don't Forget God Loves You Unconditionally

God loves you, not because of what you do, but because of who you are. And that's amazing, because if you're anything like me, you doubt, you get discouraged, you fight with the people you love, you give in to peer pressure to be accepted, you make excuses for your behavior, and you selfishly choose to go your own way, rather than trusting and following God's plan for you. And yet . . . *God still loves you for who you are.*

35

To really experience the kind of freedom God wants us to have, you'll need to believe that God loves you just as you are, not because of who you have the potential to become. When one of my daughters skinned her knee as a child, did I yell, "You stupid kid! You are the dumbest child in all of California!"? Of course not! I picked her up and reminded her that everyone stumbles and falls as they learn to walk.

The unconditional love of God is expressed beautifully in this story about what happened when Jesus met a woman who had been caught in sexual sin:

> Jesus went to the Mount of Olives. At dawn he appeared again in the temple courts, where all the people gathered around him, and he sat down to teach them. The teachers of the law and the Pharisees brought in a woman caught in adultery. They made her stand before the group and said to Jesus, "Teacher, this woman was caught in the act of adultery. In the Law Moses commanded us to stone such women. Now what do you say?" They were using this question as a trap, in order to have a basis for accusing him.
>
> But Jesus bent down and started to write on the ground with his finger. When they kept on questioning him, he straightened up and said to them, "Let any one of you who is without sin be the first to throw a stone at her." Again he stooped down and wrote on the ground.
>
> At this, those who heard began to go away one at a time, the older ones first, until only Jesus was left, with the woman still standing there. Jesus straight-

ened up and asked her, "Woman, where are they? Has no one condemned you?"

"No one, sir," she said.

"Then neither do I condemn you," Jesus declared. "Go now and leave your life of sin."

John 8:1–11

What a story! Now, in case you didn't know, in the culture back then, you could be punished by having people throw big heavy rocks at you, over and over until you died. What a terrible way to go! So, picture for a moment all those men holding rocks in their hands, ready to kill this woman for having a sexual relationship with someone she wasn't married to. (By the way, I've always wondered what happened to the man in this story who was doing the same thing. It seems like they should have brought him to Jesus too!) What did they think Jesus would say? After all, the law at that time gave them the right to kill her. But Jesus simply looked into their angry eyes and said, "Let any one of you who is without sin be the first to throw a stone at her." This was brilliant! Jesus knew they had also missed the mark of God's righteousness. They all turned around and left. He made His point loud and clear.

As the story continues, we hear a warm conversation between a woman who had sinned with her sexuality and the Lord who had every right to punish her. Instead, He showed kindness and deep compassion with a large dose of unconditional love. He asked her where her accusers were. She probably looked around just to make sure, and then told him no one was left.

Then Jesus showed the world the true character of God's love when He said, "Then neither do I condemn you." Did Jesus say her sin was okay? Not at all. In fact, He told her to leave her life of sin. But the words "neither do I condemn you" are the same words He says to us even now. He loves you completely and unconditionally, no matter what you've done.

Far too many people make a commitment to sexual integrity and then they mess up. They miss the mark with their body, eyes, mind, or heart. And sometimes they feel so ashamed or defeated that they try to break their relationship with God. But God never stops loving us. His love is strong . . . always. It's our love that wavers, not His. Notice that Jesus didn't break His relationship with that woman who was caught in the act of adultery. Instead, He told her to leave her life of sin because He knew what would be best for her. That story is an incredible picture of God's unconditional love and grace.

Here is a fact that should be written permanently in our minds: "God demonstrates his own love for us in this: While we were still sinners, Christ died for us" (Romans 5:8). If you ever doubt God's love for you, just remember what He did on the cross. I am convinced that even if you were the only person who ever lived, Jesus would still have sacrificed His life for you so that you could have a relationship with God.

Here's what is mind-blowing about God's love for you. His love is not because of what you do but because of who you are. You are His child. His ways are not like our ways. God's grace and mercy are never turned off. They are strong and constant, like a waterfall. I live in California, and we have one of the most beautiful national parks in all the world, Yosemite National

Park. The waterfalls are amazing. One day I was climbing to the top of one of those waterfalls. It was breathtaking. I looked at my watch and it was 2:00 p.m. And then it struck me that the amazing force of water toppling over the mountain and down to the floor of Yosemite below was unstoppable. It would be just as powerful at 2:00 a.m. when no one was on the trail as it was when I was standing there. God's love for you knows no limits or boundaries, and that's amazing. In the next chapter, we will see how these four amazing principles can give us a foundation for a life of healthy sexuality.

DISCUSSION STARTERS

Think about your answers to the questions below and talk about them with an adult you trust.

1. Do you believe it is possible to "lead with love" and "practice kindness" even if you disagree with a person's lifestyle or their belief about sexuality?

2. "So God created human beings in his own image. In the image of God he created them; male and female he created them" (Genesis 1:27 NLT). Do you believe this verse in the Bible? How does your answer to that question influence your thoughts about sexuality?

3. What does it mean for your life if God is the "Master Designer"? What do you think your response to that should be?

4. Why do you think it can be difficult for us to believe that God loves us unconditionally? Why is God's unconditional love such amazing news?

THREE

THE CODE

In its simplest form, a code is a way of life. We all live by certain codes of life and behavior, whether we call them that or not. For example, one of my personal codes is: *Have serious fun.* That phrase is always imbedded in my mind. It doesn't mean that I have serious fun every moment of the day, but it's a code I try to follow. Another code I live by is: *Never pass up an incredible dessert.* That phrase is also imbedded in my mind, and if I'm trying to be healthy, that code could cause a problem! These are small examples, but there are many more life-changing and important codes to follow. When it comes to sex and sexuality, there's something I call the "Sexual Integrity Code." Because I am a Christian and the Bible (God's Word) is my ultimate authority, I came up with "The Code."

The Sexual Integrity Code

In honor of God, my family, and the future He has planned for me, I commit (with God's help) to live my life with sexual integrity.

This involves

- Honoring God with my body
- Renewing my mind for good
- Turning my eyes from worthless things
- Guarding my heart above all else

Let's break this up to better understand it.

In honor of God, my family, and the future God has planned for me . . .

At some time in your life, you will decide if you're going to commit your life to God. When I was sixteen years old, I asked Jesus Christ into my life, and that was the most important decision I've ever made. So, I want to try to honor God with every decision I make about my life. I decided that I'd be most likely to live out God's purpose for my life if I follow His direction for my life. Jesus was once asked an important question, "What is the most important commandment?" Without hesitation He said, "'Love the Lord your God with all your heart and with all your soul and with all your mind and with all your strength'" (Mark 12:30). Because we're human, we're not perfect. There are times we'll miss the mark when it comes to honoring God. But loving God with all our heart, soul, mind, and strength seems like the very best place to start.

At your age, and even at mine, it's impossible to know what your future holds. Maybe you'll get married, or maybe you won't. Maybe you'll have no kids, or maybe you'll have seven! Maybe you'll travel the world, or maybe you'll live your whole life in one place you love. There's no way to predict everything that will happen. We can't know what your future holds, but we do know who holds your future. You can trust that God loves you and has an amazing plan for your life. Adding the phrase "and the future God has planned for me" is simply a way to acknowledge your relationship to Him and your future.

I commit (with God's help) to live my life with sexual integrity.

Making a commitment to anything is something that should be taken seriously because it involves dedicating yourself to something, someone, a cause, or a code of life. We make all kinds of commitments to things, but a commitment to sexual integrity is an incredibly wise choice. I just don't see a downside. Now the very next phrase is "with God's help" because sticking to a commitment to sexual integrity won't always be easy. The temptations are all around us, and by saying the words "with God's help," we're acknowledging that we can't do this on our own. We need the Master Designer of our sexuality to help us. "With God's help" is probably a phrase we should use much more often. The next phrase, "to live my life with sexual integrity," is what the Code is all about. Sexual integrity is our goal, our plan, and for most of us, the sincere desire of our heart. Living with sexual integrity means having a clear understanding of why God created sex. But it's also about respecting the power of sexuality in our own lives and the lives of others. Someone once said, "Sexual integrity is having sexual strength to do the right thing, even when others aren't looking." The next four phrases are the way I would describe how to live with sexual integrity.

1. Honor God with Your Body
   "You were bought at a price. Therefore honor God with your bodies" (1 Corinthians 6:20). The

context of this verse refers to Jesus offering His body on the cross to pay the price and take the punishment for our sin. There is no greater sacrifice than Jesus Christ, God's son, dying on the cross so that we could have eternal life. So, how should we respond? We honor God with our bodies, not just our sexuality, but giving God our very lives. However, an important part of our body is our sexuality. Here is what another scripture says: "The body, however, is not meant for sexual immorality, but for the Lord, and the Lord for the body" (1 Corinthians 6:13).

2. Renew Your Mind for Good

"Do not conform to the pattern of this world but be transformed by the renewing of your mind. Then you will be able to test and approve what God's will is—his good, pleasing and perfect will" (Romans 12:2). Your imagination and ability to think make your mind the most powerful part of your body! I tell people all the time, your most powerful sex organ is your mind! And because our minds are so powerful, they can determine the direction and quality of our lives. No matter what age, you can learn to starve your mind of harmful stuff and feed it good things instead. People who fill their mind with inappropriate pictures, videos, social media, thoughts of others, or even conversations will have a very difficult time living out sexual integrity. When we can protect our minds from those negative influences, we can, as the Scripture in Romans says, live by God's good and perfect will.

Here's a story to help you understand what I'm talking about: A man met with a counselor to talk about a dream he kept having. He kept dreaming about two cats that kept fighting. The counselor asked, "Well, who wins the fight?" The man answered, "Whichever cat I feed the most."

There is an ongoing fight inside of each and every one of us. There's the part of us that wants to follow God's plan for our lives and make wise choices. But there's also the part of us that is tempted to be selfish or sneaky and make unwise choices. And sometimes it can feel like those two things are at war inside us. And you will decide which one wins. Because the one you feed is the one that wins. When you do things like lying, looking at inappropriate pictures or videos, or sneaking around to hang out with friends who don't share your values, you're feeding the part of you that wants to make unwise choices. But when you do things like praying, reading your Bible, or talking about your struggles with a trusted adult, you're feeding the part of you that wants to make wise choices. This is what I mean when I talk about filling your mind with truth. If you put good things into your mind, good things will win out. In fact, the Bible says peace will come: "Finally, my brothers and sisters, always think about what is true. Think about what is noble, right, and pure. Think about what is lovely and worthy of respect. If anything is excellent or worthy of praise, think about those kinds of things. . . . The God who gives peace will be with you" (Philippians 4:8–9 NIRV).

The opposite happens when you "feed" your mind bad things. In chapter 7, we'll talk more about this idea of "garbage in/garbage out."

I want to challenge you to spend time each day, even a few minutes, reading a devotional or section of the Bible. Listen to good music that will lift you up and keep your mind set on positive things. It's also important to find friends who share those same values, so your conversations are good and healthy. In other words, do the kinds of things that keep your mind focused on the good. Over time, these small habits will have an enormous impact on you and the choices you make.

3. Turn Your Eyes from Worthless Things

"Turn my eyes from worthless things" (Psalm 119:37).

"Your eye is a lamp that provides light for your body. When your eye is good, your whole body is filled with light" (Matthew 6:22 NLT).

These words of Jesus might be the inspiration for the saying, "Your eyes are the window to your soul." But did you know that your eyes are also a window to your brain? Your brain basically takes a picture of everything you see and stores it in your mind.

That's why it's so important to protect your eyes from harmful things. I live near the coast in Southern California, and I love going to the beach! From an early age, I've worn sunglasses to protect my eyes from the sun. In many ways, to live by the Code you have to learn to protect your eyes from unhealthy images that can sneak into your mind and stay

there—images that can take you down a negative
road. It's natural for everyone to notice sexual images. And in case you haven't noticed, they're everywhere. One piece of advice I've learned is to "bounce
your eyes," which basically just means that when you
see something inappropriate, you look away quickly.
This gives your mind less time to take a picture that
can get stuck in your mind and never be deleted. It
takes discipline to redirect your eyes from distrac-
tions, but it's always worth it and the best way to live
YOUR best life.

4. Guard Your Heart Above All Else

"Guard your heart above all else for it determines
the course of your life" (Proverbs 4:23 NLT). To use
a sports phrase, the best offense is a good defense.
This is true in the world of sports, but it's also true
when it comes to relationships. It's unquestion-
ably true with sexual integrity. The verse above is
one of the most important principles to live by for
a flourishing life. People who can learn to guard
their hearts will have much better relationships and
prevent a lot of heartache and confusion with their
sexual lives.

How can we learn to guard our hearts? Here are
four quick thoughts for you:

1. *Do all you can to get as emotionally and spiritu-
   ally healthy as you possibly can.* People who have
   healthy practices (emotional and spiritual) are the
   people who build a firm foundation to guard their
   heart.

2. *You can choose the pain of discipline or the pain of regret.* There is pain in life. But the people who practice the pain of discipline, or work hard to build healthy habits, do well. And the ones who don't choose to do that experience the pain of regret. It's a simple principle but obviously not easy.

3. *Spend regular time with God.* I don't remember what I ate last Monday for lunch, but it gives my body strength for today. Regular times with God, practicing the spiritual habits of reading the Bible, praying, and spending time with others who share your faith and values, will make a major difference in guarding your heart.

4. *Lean into "replenishing relationships."* In life we have VDPs and VIPs (Very Draining People and Very Inspiring People). If you spend your time with very draining people or those that bring you down, then guess what? You can't possibly guard your heart. It's the VIPs who will inspire you to live a better life with more integrity. I've learned that I have to stay away from compromising situations and make sure I have relationships that provide accountability for my actions. I need people in my life who will care enough to check in with me and ask hard questions about the choices I make.

Okay, let's circle back to the Code:

The Sexual Integrity Code

In honor of God, my family, and the future God has planned for me, I commit (with God's help) to live my life with sexual integrity.

This involves:

- Honoring God with my body
- Renewing my mind for good
- Turning my eyes from worthless things
- Guarding my heart above all else

On a regular basis, I personally commit to that Code. I honestly believe there are healthy and good consequences when we live by the Code. It hasn't made me more handsome. It hasn't taken away all my questions, temptations, doubts, or struggles. HOWEVER, the Code has helped me live my life, *with God's help*, to the fullest. Even if I didn't believe in God (and I do with every ounce of my being), or even if I had made extremely poor relationship mistakes, I believe the Code is the absolute best way to live. How about you?

DISCUSSION STARTERS

Think about your answers to the questions below and talk about them with an adult you trust.

1. Some people would say that living by the Sexual Integrity Code is one of the most important decisions a person could ever make. What do you think about that?

2. In the Code it says, "I commit (with God's help) . . ." Why do you think you might need God's help to live by the Code?

3. Of the four ways to live by the Code, which seems to be the most challenging?
   - Honoring God with my body
   - Renewing my mind for good
   - Turning my eyes from worthless things
   - Guarding my heart above all else

4. Why do you think it's important to spend time in healthy relationships and with God if you want to live by the Code?

FOUR

THE FOUNDATION

If you have a pulse, you will eventually think about sex. In fact, it's completely natural at your age (or any age, for that matter) to have sexual thoughts and questions. But where you get your answers and information about your view of sexuality is more important than you might think.

Here are some options:

- You could look for answers on the Internet or social media.

  Oookaaay, and yes, the Internet is an option, AND yes, experts tell us that it's the number one place students go for sex education. But let me tell you why that's a really bad idea. As you know, there are some real wackos who post on the Internet, so it will be really easy to find terrible advice. And to be perfectly honest, the Internet and the people you follow on social media do not care about you . . . not like your parents, grandparents, aunts, uncles, and small group leaders do. Looking online will give you lots of answers, but it won't give you good answers. And that's because ANYONE can put information online. They don't have to be an expert or even know what they're talking about. And even more concerning, the Internet will quickly direct you to all kinds of things (pictures, videos, etc.) that could hurt you rather than help you.

- You could ask your friends.

  I'm really big on having great friendships, but when it comes to learning all you can about your sexuality, your friends might not know as much as they think they do. They're trying to figure out the same things you are. When I was in 5th grade, a friend on my sports team told me all about how babies are made. Since absolutely no one had ever talked to me about that subject, I said something like, "No way!" He then went on to describe in detail how men and women made babies. The problem was that I totally believed him, and he was only about 75 percent right. The other 25 percent was really weird and strange and totally incorrect. It took me several years to get his lousy advice out of my mind.

- You could get your information from your public school.

  Unfortunately, the family-life or sex-education programs that most public schools offer are what I call "value-neutral education." In other words, these programs talk about things like birth control or sexual techniques, but they don't offer anything from a values or moral perspective. I truly think they mean well, but sometimes their views will go directly against your views or family values.

- You could talk with your parents or an adult you trust.

  Most of the time, this is where you're going to get the advice and help you need for an important topic like this. Even though your parents can be awkward (no offense, parents!), they care more about you than anyone else. But, if for some reason you don't feel safe with a parent, who are the trusted adults in your life? I don't know the specific people in your life, but here's what to look for in a safe adult. A trusted adult

  - Loves and cares for you
  - Gives you wise advice
  - Tells you the truth, even when it's hard to hear
  - Is a safe place to ask questions

  The trusted adults in your life might be your parents, church leaders, grandparents, teachers, aunts and uncles, small group leaders, and coaches just to name a few. So, figure out who your trusted adults are and take your questions to the right place! It might feel awkward or uncomfortable the first time you talk about this, but it will get easier! And you'll be so glad you did.

The Foundation for a Healthy Understanding of Sexuality

There is one more place to find trusted advice and answers to your questions. You can always go directly to the *source*. In the Bible, we have complete access to the Master Designer of our sexuality. Too many people make sexual decisions based on what they see in culture, a friend who is still trying to figure it out, social media, or other outside influences. But in the Bible, we find God's truth about our sexuality. We can try to figure it out on our own, or we can learn what God, the Creator and Designer of our sexuality, has to say about it. Most people make their decisions about sexuality spontaneously or "in the moment." But I think there's a better way. And to do it right, maybe we should ask, "What does the Bible say?"

What Does the Bible Say About Sex and Sexual Integrity?

Several years ago, a teenage couple came to talk with me in my office. They had been dating for a little while and had already been having sex. She didn't want to break up, but she also didn't want them to keep having sex. He didn't want to stop anything. At the end of our time together, he was pretty frustrated. He asked, "Is God some kind of grinch when it comes to sex?"

He's not alone! Lots of people misunderstand God's plan and think He must not want us to have any fun. But that couldn't be further from the truth. Don't forget, sex was God's idea! Other people think the Bible doesn't have anything to say about sexuality. These people haven't done their homework. The Bible is obviously not a sex manual, but it does contain extremely important pieces of wisdom to help us to be all God wants us to be.

Let's take a quick look at a few of the key verses from the Bible:

The Bible on Creation

The very first sentence in the Bible says, "In the beginning God created the heavens and the earth" (Genesis 1:1). If that first sentence in the Bible is true (and I believe it is), then this is a really big deal. It also means God was intimately involved in the creation of the world, but not just the world. **God created you.** In fact, later in the first chapter of Genesis, the Bible clearly states:

> So God created human beings in his own image.
>   In the image of God he created them;
>   male and female he created them.
>
> Genesis 1:27 NLT

Wow! This means we're all created in the image of God, especially concerning our moral, spiritual, and intellectual nature. This also means that God created all aspects of our lives, including our sexuality. As our Creator and Master Designer, He is smarter than us. He's the one who can see the master plan when we can only see our part of it. God created our gender and sexuality, and He can be trusted.

Not only did He create us, but I love how the Bible describes it, "God saw all that he had made, and it was *very good*" (Genesis 1:31, emphasis added). Our God is proud of His creation. Someone told me once the words *very good* in today's modern language might be described as "God saw all that He had made, and it was AWESOME." Since God created sex and views it as *very good*, doesn't it make sense that we want to listen to the Master Designer? And just like the creator of a game system knows how it works best and all the potential problems, God (as the Creator of sex) knows how it works best and wants us to understand the potential problems.

The Bible on Adultery

You've probably heard the commandment, "You shall not commit adultery" (Exodus 20:14). Adultery is when two people have a sexual relationship and at least one of them is married to someone else. You might hear it referred to as an affair. Most people today have seen lives ruined because of adultery. I can think of entire families whose lives have been changed and even devastated because of adultery. God wants the best for you. He wants to protect you from the pain of a broken relationship. He created this rule for good reason—to protect people from the pain and destruction of life and family.

The Bible on Fornication

Fornication might be a word that's new for you, so let me explain. It's an old-fashioned word. *Fornication* is when two people who are not married have sex. Paul wrote, "It is God's will that you should be sanctified: that you should avoid sexual immorality" (1 Thessalonians 4:3). Here's a quick Greek lesson: The original word for "immorality" in this verse is *pornea*. It's where we get the root word for pornography or fornication. Some Bible translations even use the word *fornication* instead of *immorality*.

Again, is God trying to mess up our fun? No way. He knows what's best for us. He loves us. But He also understands the confusion and heartache experienced by those who choose to go against His will. I wish you could hear the stories of regret I hear from students who have engaged in sexual sin. There is guilt, pain, confusion, and for some, a feeling of hopelessness. They just didn't see it coming. It breaks my heart to hear their stories, and it reminds me again that God knew what He was doing. 1 Corinthians 6:18 says, "Flee [or run away] from sexual immorality." It doesn't say "Flee from sex within marriage." God created sex to be enjoyed in a marriage relationship when both people are fully committed to each other. God doesn't say flee from sexual immorality because He is mean. He wants the best for you.

Let me add something here, and let me be loud and clear about it. If you have already made mistakes with your sexuality, God still loves you! There is nothing you could ever do to make Him love you any less. When Jesus died on the cross, He paid the price for all our sins. He offers you forgiveness and grace. God's love knows no limit. Several years ago, I had the privilege to be the pastor to marry a girl from my youth group, Elizabeth, to her husband, John.[1] Elizabeth lived by the Code until she got married. Before John met Elizabeth, John had not lived by the Code. He had regrets about the choices he made before he understood the idea of sexual integrity, but that didn't mean he couldn't still be all that God wanted him to be. John and Elizabeth's relationship was built on grace, trust, and joy. Today, they both work with students in the inner city and bring hope and healing to students with the message of the love of God.

The Bible on Being One Flesh

Matthew, who was one of Jesus's followers, spent a lot of time with Jesus during his life and ministry. And lucky for all of us, he wrote about the things he saw and heard from Jesus during that time. You can read what he wrote in the book of Matthew in the Bible. Here is a direct quote from Jesus: "'Haven't you read,' [Jesus] replied, 'that at the beginning the Creator "made them male and female," and said, "For this reason a man will leave his father and mother and be united to his wife, and the two will become one flesh"? So, they are no longer two, but one. Therefore what God has joined together, let man not separate'" (Matthew 19:4–6).

As these verses show, God sees a physical sexual relationship as sacred and special. Sex is physical, but it's also a spiritual union. The New Testament was written in the Greek language, and the word used in that scripture for "united" also means "bonded together." A sexual relationship bonds a couple together in ways that are difficult to describe. Culture today tries to convince us that sex can be casual and that no commitment is necessary. But a casual sexual relationship devalues the other person. It's focused on the other person's body and what it can do for you, rather than the oneness you experience with the soul of the other person.

There is no better example of two becoming one than when a man and woman have sexual intercourse. Sexual intercourse is as intimate as you can get, and that kind of connection is meant to be permanent. It's not something we're made to share with multiple people. Are you prepared to become one flesh with another person? It requires serious consideration *before* you find yourself in a compromising or tempting situation. Even though movies, music, and the Internet try to make it look like sex can be casual, it's just not possible. There's really no such thing as "friends with benefits" (where people who are just friends decide to have sexual experiences with each other with no commitment). In many ways, sexual experiences are like a glue that attaches us to another person. It was created to be a permanent adhesive, so it can't be easily undone and often leaves both people hurt and confused. In other words, following the Creator's design is better, safer, and God's best for our lives.

The Bible on the Human Body

As a Christian, there's no doubt that your very own body is a temple of God. In the book of 1 Corinthians, the apostle Paul wrote: "Flee from sexual immorality. All other sins a person commits are outside the body, but whoever sins sexually, sins against their own body. Do you not know that your bodies are temples of the Holy Spirit, who is in you, whom you have received from God? You are not your own; you were bought at a price. Therefore, honor God with your bodies" (1 Corinthians 6:18–20).

I'm not a theologian, but I do know that in a mysterious way, God's Holy Spirit lives within each Christian believer. Our bodies were made to give honor to God. We were each created in the image of God, so the things we do and the way we treat others show the world a picture of what God is like. After all, He created us and lives inside us. And as you read in the previous chapter, a major part of the Sexual Integrity Code is honoring God with our bodies.

There are many other verses in the Bible that focus on sex and sexuality in addition to the ones I've mentioned. God views our sexuality as very good, incredibly special, and even sacred. He wants the best for us. That's why He wants us to wait to have sex until we are married. Sex is much more than sexual intercourse. So, it's important to live a life of sexual integrity in all areas of our lives.

Building on a Solid Foundation

The foundation for a healthy sexuality comes from God's plan, which we can read about in the Bible. The decision is yours. You can follow the wisdom of God or get pulled into the current of today's culture. I hope you'll choose to believe that God's way is the right way. It is not the easiest way. You will be tempted. You'll likely see pornography, either by accident or on purpose. You'll have times when you just want to ignore the Code. You may even have struggles with same-sex attraction. You'll have moments of weakness. But God, the Creator of sexuality, told the apostle Paul, "'My grace is sufficient for you, for my power is made perfect in weakness'" (2 Corinthians 12:9). When we feel weak or tempted, we can be confident that God's power and strength can show us a way out. He can give you the strength and discipline you need to follow His Code.

Jesus told an amazing story about building your life on a solid foundation.

> "Anyone who listens to my teaching and follows it is wise, like a person who builds a house on solid rock. Though the rain comes in torrents and the floodwaters rise and the winds beat against that house, it won't collapse because it is built on bedrock. But anyone who hears my teaching and doesn't obey it is foolish, like a person who builds a house on sand. When the rains and floods come and the winds beat against that house, it will collapse with a mighty crash."
>
> Matthew 7:24–27 NLT

This is one of the most important passages I've read in my life. It tells us that wind, rain, and storms are going to come to all our lives. In other words, temptations will come our way, along with pain, hurt, and problems. But there is an answer! Those who build their house (their life) on a solid foundation will still have the storms of life, but because their foundation is built on the Rock, they will not crash. It's the people who choose to build their life's foundation on shifting sand who crash when the storms of life come their way. When it comes to all aspects of your life, including your sexuality, do all you can to build your life on a firm foundation. It's worth the effort.

DISCUSSION STARTERS

Think about your answers to the questions below and talk about them with an adult you trust.

1. In this chapter, we talked about building your life on a solid foundation, not on shifting sand. In what ways do you think getting information about sex from the Internet or your friends could be an example of building a foundation on sand?
2. Who are the trusted adults in your life who
   • Love and care for you
   • Give you wise advice
   • Tell you the truth, even when it's hard to hear
   • Provide a safe place to ask questions
   Make a plan to talk about this book with them this week.
3. The very best way to learn about healthy sexuality is from the Master Designer Himself. After reading the

Bible verses in this chapter, what's your impression about God and His plan for healthy sexuality?

4. Why do you think God cares so much about our bodies, our minds, and our relationships?

FIVE

CULTURE, GENDER, AND AUTHORITY

There is no question that our world is deeply, deeply divided on the issues of sexuality and gender. And, I might add—a bit confused. This chapter will not resolve every issue. The voices on every side of sexuality and gender issues can be loud and forceful. If you are on social media, then you know what I mean. Everybody is an "expert," and by that, I mean that actually no one is an expert. So, which voice do you listen to, and how can you know what's true?

I'm sure that some people skipped chapters 1 through 4 to come straight to this chapter. I get it. It's a sensitive topic for everyone, and there are a lot of strong feelings on every side. But wherever you land on the subject, I only ask that you read the entire chapter. And it might be a good idea to review the four principles in chapter 2: *Always Lead with Love*, *Kindness Matters*, *You Are Created in the Image of God*, and *God Loves You Unconditionally*. Regardless of your beliefs about sexuality, lifestyle, or mindset, those principles offer the right perspective to approach this subject. I know. God's ways are different than our ways.

For topics like these, I wish we could sit at a local coffee shop and talk, rather than you just reading this book. We could discuss and interact on these important issues. If you're wrestling with any of the issues in this chapter, you are not alone. There are thousands of students in the same boat, and the most important piece of advice I can give you is, "Don't suffer in silence." Talk with a trusted adult about the issues that are bothering you.

Honestly, more than any of the other chapters in this book, I'm approaching this chapter with humility and compassion. And if we were at that coffee shop, I hope you would experience me as approachable and understanding.

Lane Shift Ahead[1]

From where I am sitting right now, I can hear the cars and trucks rolling along the 5 Freeway here in Southern California. My office is next to this incredible road that runs from the border of Mexico to the border of Canada. Last year, it seemed like there were car accidents daily, right in front of my office. I'd hear the screech of tires, then I'd cringe and wait for the sound of cars colliding. It really was out of control. It was crazy! There was a lot of road construction, and I finally realized the road had a new curve right in front of my office. People would fail to pay attention, miss the curve, and plow into another car in the other lane. Finally, authorities put up a sign, "Lane Shift Ahead." There has still been an occasional accident, but the warning sign did the trick. There has been a "lane shift" in the landscape when it comes to the rapidly changing culture surrounding sexuality and gender. I'm not sure anyone saw it coming so quickly or so forcefully. Well, truthfully, the shift in our culture isn't going away anytime soon. So, it's time to really take a look at these issues and figure out the best way to live—and which voices to trust.

Culture and Its Changing Opinions

Let me worry aloud for a moment. Culture is one of the loudest voices when it comes to sexuality and gender. But does our culture really have the answers? I'm not sure it does. In fact, as a guy quite a bit older than you, I've witnessed some huge cultural changes in sexuality and gender during my lifetime. So, if it's true that culture is constantly changing, how can it be a dependable and trustworthy guide? Some of the most common conversational topics today were almost never talked about until just a few years ago. And while it's important to be able to talk about anything, it's crucial to hear from voices that share your faith and values because God's truth is timeless.

Let's talk about two phrases we hear from some in the culture that concern me:

1. "Casual sex is okay as long as it's consensual."

   We live in a culture where "friends with benefits" is a popular idea, whether people are straight, gay, or bisexual. One study of more than a million people using Tinder (the social media app known for quick "hookups" and "hyper sexuality") found that these users were significantly more depressed and anxious. Now, that could mean that depression and anxiety make a person more likely to engage in careless sexual experiences. Or it could mean that intimately sharing your body with someone who isn't committed to you leads to depression and anxiety. Either way, the people in your life who truly care about you don't want any of those things for you. Casual sex devalues the other person. And this is always what happens when you care more about the pleasure you can get from someone, rather than respecting and honoring them for being a person who is made in the image of God. I've told people for years, "Never trade temporary pleasure for permanent regret." Sexual relationships are simply not casual. There is a certain bonding that happens with this kind of intimacy. People who focus on casual sex focus on the body and not the soul of a person. Yet, movies, shows, and social media make it look like casual sex is carefree and common. But that's just not true. I question that mentality. Viewing someone solely as a means of pleasure diminishes their worth and strips away their humanity.

2. "Do whatever you want with your sexuality."

That's just not a good idea. For example, the power of sexual relationships can trick people into what we call "Instant Intimacy." Too often people make decisions that will affect the rest of their lives just because of how they're feeling at the time, or because they've been intimate with someone. Life-long decisions based on feelings or a false sense of bonding are not the reason to make a life choice. This is true for a heterosexual or homosexual relationship. Two quick stories: A married couple with two little kids came into my office for marriage counseling. They were in a horrible place in their relationship. As it turns out, they were having sex before marriage. Because of the pleasure and intimacy they were experiencing with each other, they were fooled into thinking they were in love. But truthfully, it was only infatuation. But because they felt connected to each other, they decided to get married. They had two beautiful babies, but now their marriage was having major problems. A few years into marriage, the feelings had worn off, and the reality was that neither of them really loved the other. Today they are divorced, and their kids are still struggling.

My second story is about a fourteen-year-old girl. I'll call her Grace. Most of her friends were talking about gender identity and trying to figure out what pronoun to choose. They were in what I would call an "experimental phase" of their life. Grace began to feel pressured by her friends to change her pronouns and to be nonbinary. Most of her friends were identifying as bisexual, and at fourteen, most of these girls were experimenting with some degree of sexual behavior with their friends, mainly other girls. Grace hadn't thought much about this until just recently. Looking back, she realized that she had experienced some depression and anxiety as she desperately wanted to be accepted by this group of friends. So, one night at an all-girls sleepover, she started kissing and fondling one of her friends. Since the pleasure felt great, she assumed she was a lesbian. Grace began to tell people she was nonbinary and leaning toward being a lesbian. Her friends embraced her newfound sexuality, and she even got affirmation from a teacher at school she really liked.

Two years later after some healthy counseling, Grace decided that in her search to be accepted by friends and find her identity, she had misjudged those first experiences. She decided that she was *not* nonbinary or a lesbian, but instead she was straight. She made a courageous decision to see things differently than some of her peers and began to tell people she was heterosexual. To be honest there were some consequences to her decision, and she lost some friends over it. Because of everything that happened, Grace had some past sexual baggage to deal with, and she suffered emotional consequences for some of her past choices. Even today, she still struggles with anxiety sometimes. But she's getting stronger every day as she develops new friendships and a vibrant faith.

Are you going to choose the ever-changing culture to be your greatest influence?

I was talking recently with a well-known Christian leader about a conversation he had with a young woman about her sexuality and gender. She told him that two weeks prior, her best friend had decided she was gay. This young woman had recently been watching some TikTok videos that had convinced her to experiment with her sexuality and gender identity. My friend, in the most loving way he could, asked, "Will you let your friend's decision two weeks ago and Tik-Tok influence your decision about sexual integrity?" He went on to say, "Why would someone prioritize their friend's recent thoughts and the cultural impact of social media over the trusted and time-tested influence of Scripture that has guided us for thousands of years?" My friend was asking some very important questions.

Here are my thoughts on culture and sexuality: culture changes. And cultural thoughts on gender have changed over the years. My experience is that culture can't always be trusted, but *God is trustworthy*. Culture won't save you or bring understanding and meaning to your life, *God will*.

Culture has given us porn, sex slavery, sex trafficking, and sexual abuse, all of which get worse every year. Of the ten worldwide websites with the highest views, two of them are actually porn sites. Do you really trust YouTube, Instagram, Snapchat, and TikTok? I doubt it. I don't. When it comes down to it, we will have to ask this question: "What voices am I going to listen to when it comes to sexual integrity?" Think about the future you desire and the kind of future God has planned for you. Is your ultimate authority the ever-changing culture or God, the Creator and Designer of our sexuality? The way I look at it, following the Creator's design is safer and better for us.

Some students say that they're not influenced by culture but that they have an inner feeling that they're somehow different. Maybe they've never felt comfortable with their sexuality or sexual identity. My only suggestion is to take it slow. This is not a decision to make quickly, and you don't want to rush into making a big change. The Bible says, "Where there is no counsel the people fall but in the multitude of counselors there is safety" (Proverbs 11:14 NKJV). I'll talk more about this in another chapter, but it's always helpful to get advice and input from a trusted adult who shares your faith and values. Our feelings are real, but they can't always be trusted. I heard someone put it this way: "Emotions are like little children. We don't want them driving the car, but we can't put them in the trunk either." Our feelings and emotions were created by God, and they do influence us in many ways. But they can be ever-changing. So we can't put our feelings in the driver's seat and let them make all our decisions. The very best place for information and insight about our gender and sexuality is God. As I said before, the one who designed you is the only person who can define you. So, lean into God's Word and to the trusted adults He's put in your life.

Someone once said, "Playing God is exhausting!" When it comes to our sexuality, it's important to have faith in God as the ultimate Creator of our lives, including our sexuality and gender. This quote is worth reading twice: "Self is the new god, the new spiritual authority, the new morality. But this puts a crushing weight on the self—one it was never designed to bear."[2]

Gender

There is widespread confusion today when it comes to the concept of gender. In its simplest biological form, *gender* means male or female. Like so many other terms, that definition was consistent throughout the past centuries. It's only been in recent history where people (culture) have creatively added to the definition of *gender* by using words like "characteristics" of male and female that are "socially constructed." This has made the definition much more fluid, meaning it changes to become looser and, well, fuzzy.

This is not a book on gender. There are better resources that go into greater depth on this subject. But I would like to bring up some important concerns.

Stereotypes

Jackie Hill Perry is an amazing woman with an amazing story.[3] Her book *Gay Girl, Good God* tells her story. Thousands of people have been helped by her message of hope and healing. Growing up, Jackie didn't fit the stereotype of a girl the way culture defines it. She didn't wear dresses. She didn't like pink. She didn't like "girl stuff." She claimed to like to do "guy things" that in her mind were more popular with guys than girls. In a time of confusion in her life, she decided because she wasn't like other girls, she must be gay. She was getting the message that if she didn't fit the stereotype of girlhood defined by culture, she should question herself, rather than question the stereotype. Today, Jackie is a spokesperson on behalf of seeking God's authority over stereotypes.

Jason is a dancer. He never liked baseball, basketball, football, or soccer. Jason loved music, art, and dance. Kids made fun of him growing up because he didn't fit the stereotype. They figured he was gay or would one day be trans. Jason began a romantic relationship with another guy who was very similar to himself. He finally felt accepted by someone. He loved the attention and, frankly, the pleasure. Jason's parents didn't approve of this relationship, and they weren't being loving at all. Jason called them "homophobic" because they were unkind to gay people. He said his parents would admit that they themselves were sinners, but they believed that homosexuality was on a whole different level of sin. In their mind his relationship with another guy was a greater sin. Jason's relationship didn't last. His partner cheated on him, and soon it was over. By the way, research indicates that same-sex relationships generally do not last as long as relationships between a man and woman.

Jason was part of a professional dance company. One of the women in the dance company was Allison, who was happily married to her husband. They were always very kind to Jason, showing him lots of love and grace. They were active in their church and even invited Jason to go with them. He didn't go, but during a dinner one night with this couple, the topic of homosexuality came up. Jason asked them, "Do you believe a same-sex relationship is sin?" Jason thought their answer was insightful: "We don't believe it's a sin to experience a same-sex attraction. But we believe that, just like if we were in an adulterous relationship, we would be ignoring God's purpose for our life, and that would be a sin."[4] Jason had never thought about his sexuality in that way before. But because the voice of shame echoed so strongly in Jason's mind from his past experiences, it took him a few years and more broken relationships to be able to work through it. He was finally able to come to understand that he could enjoy dance, art, and other things that aren't stereotypical male passions and not be gay. Today he is married to an amazing woman, they have two kids, and they're active in a wonderful church. He's shared that because of his past, he still has temptations like everyone.

Developing a Sense of Identity

One of the most important tasks of the teenage years is to develop a healthy self-identity. To get to that healthy place, you will need to wrestle with some big questions. Questions like, *Who am I?* And, *How do I fit into this world?* Most teens want and need a strong sense of belonging. It's normal to experiment with different styles of music, clothing, media, friendships, and even belief in God as you figure out your true identity. Well, guess what? Your adolescent years are also a time of figuring out your sexual identity. When I was working on my graduate degree in adolescence (yeah, I studied people like you!), I learned a lot from a guy named Erik Erikson. He was an authority in adolescent behavior, and this is a summary of what he wrote concerning your stage in life: The main task of adolescents is to solve the crisis of identity versus role confusion. Research has shown that a stable and strong sense of identity is associated with better mental and emotional health in adolescents.

You see, Erikson knew there is a connection between a strong sense of identity and better mental and emotional health. I'm afraid too many teens are missing out on developing a sense of healthy identity by making early choices about their sexual identity that won't be good for them in the long run.

Don't Rush It

If you have questions, doubts, or struggles about your gender identity or sexual preferences, *don't rush it*. At your age, you are still working through many aspects of your identity. Jumping into a sexual relationship with anyone or experimenting with casual sexual experiences will only make things more complicated and confusing. I don't think that is a healthy decision, period.

Some people experience what is known as "gender dysphoria." Here is a short definition of a very complicated issue: "Gender dysphoria is a term that describes a sense of unease that a person may have because of a mismatch between their biological sex and their gender identity. This sense of unease or dissatisfaction may be so intense it can lead to depression and anxiety and have a harmful impact on daily life."[5]

Sometimes when a person is experiencing depression or anxiety, they can make hasty decisions about their sexual identity without thinking about what it will mean in the long run. Some people struggle internally but don't take the time to really process their issues or to get counseling from someone they trust. As we learn more about gender dysphoria and the incredibly huge rise among teens in the last few years, we are just beginning to see a pattern emerge. Many of these students were exposed to excessive Internet and social media. They also experienced a greater amount of depression and anxiety. Many of these young people could be better described as "gender insecure," meaning for whatever reason, they are insecure about their sexual identity. But there are studies indicating that if a student will work on getting help for their depression and anxiety, many times their gender dysphoria issues disappear.

Let me explain why I suggest we don't rush to do something rash: internal issues are not solved by external solutions. In other words, you don't want to settle a temporary issue with a permanent solution. In recent days there have been many young people who were diagnosed with gender dysphoria who began hormone treatments or sex reassignment surgery, only to change their mind later! The sex reassignment surgery was a permanent change to a temporary feeling. The external solution did not resolve the internal feeling. Even people who are transgender are encouraging students to slow down in their decisions. Did you know that the decision-making part of our brains hasn't fully developed until we are closer to twenty-five years old? Making a hasty decision can be hazardous to your life and future.

Gay, Lesbian, and Bi . . . or Straight

Because you are still forming your sexual identity, it is not a good idea to rush into same-sex relationships. To paraphrase a Bible verse, "As a person thinks in their heart, so they become" (see Proverbs 23:7). Your mind is very powerful, and we often become what we focus on all the time. It's called self-fulfilling prophecy. You don't want to label yourself to be gay, lesbian, or bisexual when you are still trying to figure out your identity. This is only going to confuse you. It is your life, and the decisions you make today will affect the rest of your life.

Authority

Ultimately, you must decide whose voice you will listen to. I'm not sure I even trust my own voice when it comes to a lot of things. I definitely don't always trust the culture. When it comes to your sexual identity you will choose who your authority is. The Bible has been incredibly helpful to me when it comes to deciding what I believe.

Here are a few Scriptures for you to think about.

> All Scripture is inspired by God and is useful to teach us what is true and to make us realize what is wrong in our lives. It corrects us when we are wrong and teaches us to do what is right.
>
> 2 Timothy 3:16 NLT

Other versions of that verse use the phrase "All scripture is 'God-breathed,'" and I love that phrase. It keeps coming back to what we believe about God doesn't it?

> So, God created human beings in his own image. In the image of God, he created them; male and female he created them.
>
> Genesis 1:27 NLT

You will have to decide whether the Master Designer is the ultimate authority for you and this world. If Genesis 1:27 is true, it does play an important part in deciding to listen to the voice of the Creator.

> "Those who accept my commandments and obey them are the ones who love me. And because they love me, my Father will love them. And I will love them and reveal myself to each of them."
>
> John 14:21 NLT

These words come directly from the mouth of Jesus. There is a lot packed into this one verse from the Bible. Jesus is telling us that if you say you love Him, then you will obey Him. Not only that, but it's through our obedience that God reveals His will for us. We love Him, we obey Him, and He reveals Himself to us.

As I study people who walk away from God or choose to listen to another voice, here are two insightful thoughts that I heard my pastor, Jeff Maguire, mention: "Whenever beliefs do not match behaviors, people change their beliefs to match their behavior." Another way of saying it is, "Whenever moral intentions do not match actual behavior, people modify their morality to accommodate behavior."[6]

I know those two quotes are a mouthful, but this is what has happened in our culture today. People are putting their own self ahead of the authority of God and then changing their beliefs. That is not a healthy way to live life.

Here is what I believe:

- You are uniquely created and designed by God.
- Every single person is made in the image of God.
- God loves you and wants the best for you.
- The Bible is our authority for life.
- God's authority doesn't change.
- We cannot trust our feelings over the authority of God.
- Everyone can have universal access to God but not universal affirmation for their life choices.
- Even if you follow the Sexual Integrity Code, your life will not be perfect.

Ultimately, you will decide what to do with your sexual integrity. As I mentioned at the beginning of this chapter, this is not *the* conclusive book on culture, gender, or authority. If this is a struggle for you, then I strongly urge you to seek wisdom and counsel from a trusted adult. And if you are a Christian, look to God's wisdom.

There is much discussion and debate in our world today about these topics. After years of dealing with the issues of culture, gender, and authority, I am in complete agreement with Dr. Preston Sprinkle's[7] perspective on marriage. So, here's a quote from him I'd like to share with you from his film series on Christian sexuality. "We believe God created marriage to be between one man and one woman and all sexual relationships outside of his covenant bond of marriage is sin, including same-sex relationships. And yet, we also passionately believe God loves and values gay people."

I guess it really does come down to these questions: "Whose voice are you going to listen to?" and "What are you going to do with what God says?" I know those sound like simple questions, but they are far from simple.

DISCUSSION STARTERS

Think about your answers to the questions below and talk about them with an adult you trust.

1. Some people will say that this chapter was "controversial." Why do you think they might call it that and is there anything you would have added to this chapter?

2. No one would disagree that the culture is rapidly changing. Why do you think it could be a bit

dangerous to base your sexual integrity on the voice of culture?

3. What part of the section on gender did you like? Was there anything in that section that you didn't like or that brought questions to your mind? One of the suggestions was to not rush your decisions. Was that a good idea? (Make sure you talk through these issues with your trusted adult.)

4. There were two phrases in this chapter that are very important to think about: *"Whenever beliefs do not match behaviors, people change their beliefs to match their behavior"* and *"Whenever moral intentions do not match actual behavior, people modify their morality to accommodate behavior."* What are your thoughts about those two phrases?

5. Jim says the Bible is our authority for life and can be trusted. What is your belief about the Bible being your authority?

SIX

CHANGES
IN YOUR BODY

You have probably already noticed the changes happening in your body. From before you were born until this moment, your body has been changing, growing, dying, all in constant movement. But when it comes to sexuality, there is a specific kind of change called puberty.

Puberty usually happens between the ages of ten and fourteen. Some bodies change earlier and some later. I was the only kid at Horace Mann Elementary School who had hair underneath their arms in fourth grade. Well, actually there was a girl named Priscilla who did too, but that's another story. Some girls develop sooner than others, and for some it happens a little more slowly. One remarkable thing about the human body is that it all works out in the end! When you're thirty years old, it won't matter when you started or completed puberty. But when you're in the midst of all those changes, it can feel like a VERY big deal. Most kids I know don't want to stand out as the first or the last one to experience these changes—they just want to blend in with everyone else. But no matter when it happens, it's important to understand the changes that are happening to your body. And it's totally normal to be curious and to have questions.

I'm gonna try really, really hard *not* to make this chapter feel like a science class. Plus, I'm not a biology expert. In fact, I took high school biology in the summer because I heard it was easier! This chapter might feel a little embarrassing because of all the talk about body parts, but it's much too important to ignore it. Eventually everyone has to talk about these things, so it might as well be now.

I mentioned that I have three daughters. Each of them reacted differently to this information when they were around your age. One of them was totally into the conversation. She asked lots of questions. Even though it felt awkward and embarrassing to me, the conversation was engaging and encouraging. My next daughter listened quietly with wide eyes and then said, "Can we just stop this conversation right now?" Our youngest daughter informed us that she already knew this stuff because her sisters had explained everything in detail to her—with drawings! Yikes.

There's not just one "right way" to react to this topic. Everyone is different! But the information is important, even though some of the words and the drawings are a bit embarrassing. (Sorry.)

Guys and Girls Are Created Differently

Physically and emotionally, things are changing quickly. Your body and your mind are going through some major changes and growth spurts. And while some of the changes that guys and girls experience are similar, they do approach sexuality and relationships very differently. That's why your commitment to sexual integrity is extremely important at this stage of your life.

Just last night as I was coming home from work, I noticed a neighbor girl hugging and kissing a guy at the park near our house. Only three months ago we were at her house, and she told me she wasn't interested in boys yet. A lot can change in three months!

My pastor used to say, "God is never too early, and He is never too late." Regardless of how you feel about puberty, it shows up right on time for each person. And it can be helpful to learn what to expect when that happens. The changes are unique for each person, but basic things will happen to your body and emotions that are similar to what's happening to your friends. As we look at these changes and differences between guys and girls, remember that God is the Master Designer who has created every detail of your body. He's also the one who designed it to develop over time. From the day you were just a little collection of cells in your mother's womb, God was looking out for you. And as you read this chapter, keep in mind what David said in the book of Psalms: "For you created my inmost being; you knit me together in my mother's womb. I praise you because I am fearfully and wonderfully made; your works are wonderful; I know that full well. My frame was not hidden from you when I was made in the secret place, when I was woven together in the depths of the earth. Your eyes saw my unformed body" (Psalm 139:13–16).

Emotional Changes

Guys, we'll start with you first. Guys typically develop later than girls, both emotionally and sexually. When I was twelve, I was still really short and had a huge crush on Sue Stonestreet, who was really tall. We were the same age, but she had already grown and developed into a young woman while I still had a squeaky voice and stood about six inches shorter than her. She saw me as a squirrelly, awkward boy, so she obviously had no interest in me. But hey, I could dream!

Guys your age are very physical. You can see that in the way lots of guys like to wrestle around with friends. Actually, that's evidence of the natural craving guys have for physical connection. And that's not bad. We were all born with the desire to feel physically close to people we care about. So, sometimes you're physical with your eyes and even with your hands. In general, guys have an easier time separating or disconnecting what their body is doing from their mind, heart, and soul. Believe me, this can get you into trouble. In fact, when it comes to sexuality, guys will often give love to get sex. They are stimulated or motivated by what their eyes see, and they want more!

Girls, on the other hand, are typically more emotional. Many girls going through puberty experience a lot of emotions and drama in their relationships. Relationship drama can be with friends, as well as with guys they find attractive, and that's a natural part of life. Girls crave emotional connection. A girl's body, unlike most guys' bodies, is extremely connected to their mind, heart, and soul. Girls, too, often give sex to get love. That's just the opposite of what we said about guys, who will often give love to get sex. Girls today can be visually stimulated like guys, but they are much more

84

moved through words, affectionate touch, and romance—in other words, things that connect to their emotions.

Women are excited sexually primarily by what they hear, and men are excited primarily by what they see. Is either way wrong? Not necessarily. They are just different. The earlier you understand the differences, the more informed and aware you will be as you consider living your life with sexual integrity. Footnote: Most people would agree with me about these "gender generalizations," but please understand that these examples are not always the case. Each person is unique and deals with puberty and gender differently.

When I talked with my daughters about these differences, I tried to help them understand how certain clothing choices could be making it more difficult for the guys in their lives. We know guys are excited sexually by what they see. But this was a hard concept for my daughters to understand because they're girls and girls don't think like guys. At the same time, when I talk with guys about girls and their need for emotional involvement, sometimes it feels like I'm speaking another language entirely. They just don't understand. It reminds me of a book that came out many years ago called *Men Are from Mars, Women Are from Venus*. That title is a good illustration of how guys and girls can approach relationships and their sexuality very differently. And if you think figuring all this out is easy, forget it. I've been married a very long time, and I'm still learning!

Physical Differences

Okay, this time I'll start with the girls. And just a head's up . . . here come those drawings I warned you about!

85

As I have studied the human body systems and especially the reproductive (or sexual) systems, I am amazed at how God, our Master Designer, thought of everything. The entire system was created with you and me in mind. It is beautiful, intricate, practical, and in many situations, enjoyable.

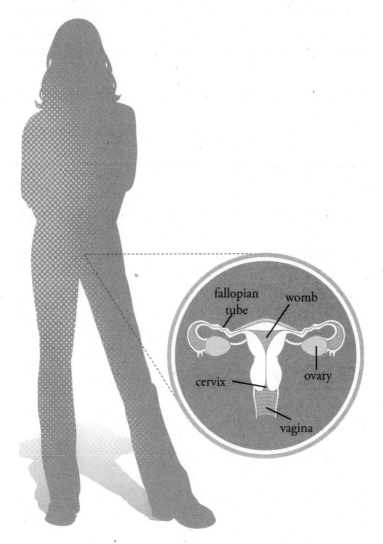

I have a very good friend who is a gynecologist, and she tells me that most girls really don't understand their sexual systems when they come in to visit her for the first time. She also says that while delivering thousands of babies, most dads don't have a clue about the female sexual system, much less their own. So here is an explanation of the sexual systems—females first. I do want to mention though, that there are other books available for a much more detailed look at the physiological and biological specifics of female and male bodies. Remember, I'm the guy who barely understood this stuff in biology class.

One of the first visual changes in a young woman's body is a growth in breast size and broadening of the hips. Before puberty, a girl's chest and a guy's chest look pretty much the same. But when puberty happens, that begins to change. No matter the size, breasts have two parts: *milk glands* that connect to the nipples through tiny tubes, and *fatty tissues* that make the breasts soft. As much as culture today might focus on the size of breasts, God's plan was to produce an efficient way to feed a baby. And that can happen regardless of breast size. A female's hips will typically grow wider, and hair begins to grow in the pubic area (the front part of the body that your underwear covers) and under the arms. All this is natural and usually welcomed by young girls as a sign their bodies are developing.

A woman has a pair of *ovaries* that begin to come alive in a different way at puberty. There are thousands of under-developed *egg cells* stored in the ovaries, and somewhere between the ages of ten and thirteen, the ovaries begin to produce *estrogen*. Estrogen is a hormone that helps control the many changes going on inside your body. Approximately once a month, after puberty, the ovaries release an egg. This is called *ovulation*. The egg moves into the *fallopian tubes*, which connect the ovaries to the uterus. The fallopian tubes are the pathway for the egg to travel to the womb. They are also the place where the male sperm and female egg meet to create a baby. (I'll come back to that in a minute.) The *uterus* is also called the womb, and that is where a baby grows until it's born. When an egg is not fertilized (no sperm is present to fertilize the egg), it moves down to the uterus. Every month, a woman's body begins to line the uterus with blood to prepare a soft and safe place for a fertilized egg to grow. And if the egg is not fertilized, it will pass through without stopping and that soft lining of blood will leave the body through the vagina. That is what is happening when a woman has her period.

The *vagina* is a passageway from the uterus to the outside of your body. During birth, the vagina is also the birth canal. It is a three- to four-inch tube made of muscle that can stretch. During sexual intercourse, the vagina expands and lubricates itself to make things easier and more enjoyable. As you can probably see, everything has a purpose and is connected in one way or another. The vagina is connected to the *cervix,* which is a strong muscle that separates the vagina from the uterus. The main job of a cervix is to create a kind of plug when a woman gets pregnant. The cervix protects the fluid sac around the baby in the womb.

Okay, how are we doing? Are you confused yet? Let's keep going—we're almost done with this part!

The next part of the sexual system is connected to the vagina. Next to the vaginal opening is the *urethra.* The urethra is located in front of and totally separate from the vaginal canal, and it is the passageway that allows urine to exit the body. The *labia* are two different sets of skin folds to protect the vagina. The *clitoris* is a very small organ located toward the front of a woman's vagina with tissue that works as a nerve ending for sexual pleasure. As you can see, the sexual system of a female is complicated and there are lots of different parts. But every single part was created by God. He thought of everything! He cares about every part of us and wants us to understand and enjoy our bodies in the commitment and security of marriage.

Okay, now let's move on to the guys, and then we'll come back to reproduction.

Typically, the first outward sign of a young man who is beginning the journey of puberty is that *hair* will begin to grow above the penis. Since everybody develops at different ages and stages, a guys' locker room can be a bit intimidating because some guys will have hair, and some will not. The next thing that happens is the *penis* and *scrotum* will have a growth spurt. Just like breasts, penises are different sizes for everyone.

The penis is made up of soft tissue, and it basically has three parts. The *shaft* is the longer part and is connected to the head or *glans*. The glans has very smooth and sensitive skin that is a bit different from the shaft of the penis. There is a hole at the end of the glans where the man passes urine and sperm. We will get to the sperm in a minute. The other part of the penis is what is called the *foreskin*. The foreskin is a continuation of the skin on the shaft that covers the glans. Some guys had their foreskin removed when they were first born. This is called *circumcision*. Jewish boys and most American boys are circumcised. Some other cultures do not practice circumcision. In our culture today, it's typically a matter of parental choice. Both ways are totally normal.

Hanging below the penis is a sac-like part of a man's body called the *scrotum*. The scrotum houses two key parts of the male sexual system called testes or testicles. They are

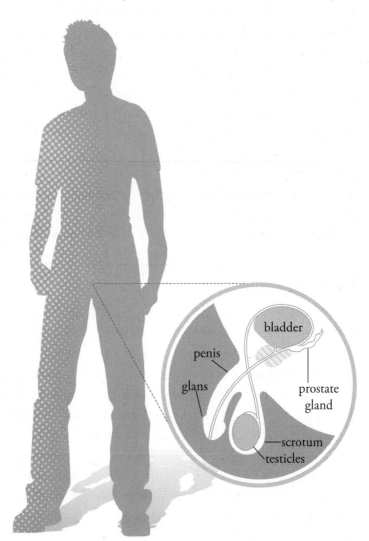

two small egg-shaped organs that have two very important functions: The testicles produce *testosterone*, which is the hormone that increases muscle development, causes hair to grow in new places, and makes the voice sound deeper. The other function of the testicles is the production of *sperm,* which is needed to fertilize a woman's egg and create a child. As young men reach puberty, their testicles begin to produce about one hundred million sperm every day. The testosterone in a man's body helps the *prostate gland* and other glands produce fluid. That fluid mixes with the sperm to come out of a man's body when he has an *ejaculation*. An ejaculation is the process during sexual stimulation when a male's penis becomes firm, and *semen* comes out. Semen is a white milky substance that is a mixture of sperm and other fluids from those male glands. When your birth dad's sperm and your birth mom's egg met after sexual intercourse, you were created!

Pregnancy

Okay, let's clear up one thing: you were not delivered to your parents by a stork! As I mentioned earlier, the Bible is quite clear about human sexuality.

At many Christian wedding ceremonies, a Scripture is read to the couple. It's found in the Old Testament, and Jesus quoted it in the New Testament. He said, "For this reason a man will leave his father and mother and be united to his wife, and the two will become one flesh" (Matthew 19:5). Although this verse is talking about much more than just sexual intercourse, it's an illustration of two people becoming one.

When a man and woman experience sexual intercourse, two bodies have literally become one. In a loving marriage, the experience of sexual intercourse should be a wonderful feeling. It brings two people who have committed their lives together to become one. The feeling can be incredibly enjoyable. During intercourse, the penis is firm and goes inside the vagina. When ejaculated, between two hundred and six hundred million sperm are released inside the woman's vagina. You can almost imagine the sperm "swimming" like fish through the vaginal canal, cervix, and uterus into the fallopian tube where, at a certain time of the month, the woman's egg will greet the sperm that have survived this long journey. (Most of the sperm will die before getting to the fallopian tubes.) The sperm and egg unite, and the sperm fertilizes the egg. At this amazingly miraculous moment, a baby is conceived.[1]

Personally, I believe that when an egg is fertilized, it is one of the most remarkable miracles of God. It's the beginning of a baby's life. You can see through these illustrations what developments are happening for that new baby growing inside a mother's womb. And, yes, a baby can look pretty strange in the first two weeks—a bit like an alien from outer space, if we're being honest. But the amazing part is that by week four or five, the baby's heart is already beating with a regular rhythm.

Okay, we got through this chapter. I hope it wasn't a horrible experience, and I'm guessing you might have learned something. I didn't know most of this stuff until after I got married. But let's move on. And I promise there will be no more semi-cheesy diagrams.

DISCUSSION STARTERS

Think about your answers to the questions below and talk about them with an adult you trust.

1. What did you learn from the description of what happens during puberty?
2. What sounded exciting about puberty? What sounded a little scary?
3. What part of this chapter is most helpful? Which part feels the most awkward to talk about?
4. Pregnancy is an incredible miracle of God. Why do you think God would use sexuality as a part of the creation of babies?

SEVEN

THE BATTLE FOR YOUR MIND

Many years ago, a man was traveling across the country by sneaking from one freight train to the next. One night, he climbed into what he thought was an ordinary boxcar and closed the door. It automatically locked shut and trapped him inside. When his eyes adjusted to the light, he realized he was inside a refrigerated boxcar and quickly became aware of the intense, freezing cold. He undoubtedly called for help and pounded on the door, but he couldn't get anyone's attention. After many hours of struggle, he lay down on the floor of the railroad car.

As he tried to fight against the freezing cold, he scratched a message on the floor explaining his unfortunate, imminent death. Late the next day, repairmen from the railroad opened the door and found the dead man inside. Though the man looked like he had frozen to death, the truth was the repairmen had come to fix the broken refrigerator unit in that car.

Most likely the temperature of the railroad car had never fallen below fifty degrees during the night. The man died because he *thought* he was freezing to death.

Variations of this story have been published in different places, so I'm not sure of its accuracy, but there's no doubt that the mind is a very powerful thing. In fact, your thoughts have a major influence in nearly every aspect of your life. The Bible says, "As he [a man] thinks in his heart, so is he" (Proverbs 23:7 NKJV). The philosopher Ralph Waldo Emerson is said to have written, "Man becomes what he thinks about all day long."

In fact, your mind is your most important sex organ! And what you put into your mind will most often determine if you win or lose with sexual integrity. My dad used to say, "If you put garbage into your mind, garbage will come out. If you put good things into your mind, good things will come out." Life is an echo: you get back what you put into it. If you plant negative thoughts and images, what do you think will grow inside your mind? So, if you want to live a healthy, positive life of sexual integrity, you will need to control what you allow to enter your mind.

Because of our sex-obsessed culture, it's very easy to slip into thinking about sexuality in a negative, unhealthy way. I remember a time watching a PG-13 movie with my wife. In the movie, the hero was married to an evil, bitter woman. As the movie progressed, he met a sweet, kind woman, and I found myself hoping he would dump his wife and go with the other woman. I couldn't believe I was actually cheering for adultery. The man was tempted, but in the end, he stayed true to his morals and remained with his wife. When it was over, I realized I was hoping for something that would break one of the Ten Commandments. It's so easy to go in the wrong direction with our minds and compromise our values if we let our thoughts go in any direction other than integrity.

Powerful Influences

You've probably already noticed, but sexual images are everywhere you look! Movies, advertising, social media, and the Internet are constantly serving up all kinds of harmful images. And these images are more common and more accessible than ever before in our history. So, if you don't stand firm about what you will and will not allow into your mind, it will be impossible to follow your moral code.

Even while writing this book, I have been trying to help a struggling college student who was raised in a Christian home. In elementary and middle school, she was a leader in her church and committed to sexual integrity. She thought she was invincible. Since then, she has walked away from her commitment to her faith and now struggles with addictions to porn and marijuana. When we talked about looking back at what happened, it was clear that it wasn't just one big thing that happened. It was lots of little compromises along the way that led to a change in her values. She lost her passion. She dropped her guard. She flirted with culture, and eventually the negative stuff in her mind pushed everything else aside. It started with choosing friends who didn't share her faith and values. Then she began choosing movies, shows, and social media influencers that were filling her mind with negative influences. She thought it wasn't a big deal that she was listening to music with inappropriate lyrics, telling her parents it was fine because she didn't listen to the words. But today, as a college dropout and an addict, she can see clearly that she was wrong about a lot of things. The thought that "It will never happen to me" is not always true. We must guard our minds by tuning out the bad stuff and tuning in the good. It will take discipline to keep your mind free of the negative and full of the positive, but with God's help, you can train yourself to do it. Paul gave Timothy some great advice: "Train yourself to be godly" (1 Timothy 4:7).

Pornography: *Caution: Pornography Is Poison to Your Mind.*

We will talk more about pornography in another chapter but let me say this: *Pornography is harmful and addictive.* It may be the greatest threat to the hearts and minds of your generation. Many well-meaning students have "flirted with pornography," thinking they could just take a quick look . . . and then another, only to lose the battle and live with major regrets. It's not an innocent thing to mess around with. Looking at pornography, even just once, is like playing with fire. I recently researched the effect that pornography has on teenagers. Do you realize that between twelve and fourteen billion dollars are spent on pornography in the United States each year?[1] A 2022 study found that 73 percent of teens ages ten to seventeen consumed online pornography.[2] And that number has doubled since 2014. Over half of all American teenagers have at least some exposure to pornography once a month. No wonder so many people struggle with their sexuality!

If you are tempted to look at pornography, even if you're just curious, don't do it. When you let those images into your mind, there's an overwhelming temptation to take it a step farther and eventually act on what you've seen. I'm on a national call-in counseling radio show called *New Life Live*, and every day we get calls from people about the negative effect their pornography addiction has on their life. It's a very strong force to try to fight against. The people I know who have struggled with a porn addiction say the same thing— stay away from porn! What starts out innocently can lead to a strong and growing hunger for more. There is absolutely no benefit to pornography. *Pornography is poison to your mind.*

Digital Screens

I'm not going to tell you to throw out every digital screen in your house, but it's important to think about what comes into your home and your mind through your digital screens. Digital screens can be television, computer, smartphones, and any other device that brings images into your mind. The average student attends school approximately one thousand hours a year; that same student watches more than 1,500 hours of TV during the same year. When you add all kinds of social media (YouTube, TikTok, Instagram, etc.), your screens are active over five hours a day. And that number is even higher for about one fourth of the student population with ten hours a day. Of course, all social media or TV isn't bad, but the impact on our minds is HUGE. The average student will see thousands of sexual images a year. Not only is that not healthy for our minds or thought life, but it can also confuse students about their sexual identity and more.

If you let your mind focus excessively on sexual images, it will absolutely have an impact on you. If you don't believe me, just think about how ads influence your lifestyle and buying habits. Advertisers aren't investing millions of dollars just to entertain you. They want to sell you products or ideas. You won't be any happier just because you buy a certain pair of jeans or drink the same brand of soft drink that a celebrity or influencer does. But the advertisements we see can certainly make us think we will!

Music Influence

You and your friends might be unified by one common interest more than any other: music. The latest surveys tell us that the average student listens to four hours of music per day, and more than 85 percent of young people in the U.S. claim rock (in one form or another) as their favorite kind of music.[3] Four hours of anything will have a profound influence on our lives and on our minds. Even if you don't realize it, your mind is recording *everything* it sees and hears.

The music that we listen to isn't all good or all bad. But we do need to be careful what music we put in our minds. It sticks with us, and whether we realize it or not, it fills our minds with thousands of thoughts. For me personally, the verse I used in an earlier chapter is especially important here: "Do not conform to the pattern of this world but be *transformed by the renewing of your mind*. Then you will be able to test and approve what God's will is—his good, pleasing, and perfect will" (Romans 12:2, emphasis added).

Whether it's the music we listen to, the movies we watch, or our social media use, it all has an influence on us. And if we choose to follow God, we'll need to constantly be aware that the spiritual discipline of renewing our minds is key to living out our Christian life.

When it comes to listening to music you have three options:

1. Don't listen to music at all.
2. Listen to anything and everything.
3. Be a selective listener.

Although many students go with option 2, I hope you won't. Studies about the subconscious mind lead me to believe it's difficult to listen to anything and everything and still live with integrity. Most teens say they don't listen to the lyrics. But when asked the words of the songs, even they are surprised at how much of a song they can repeat from memory.

Here are some excellent questions and guidelines for listening to any music:

- Does the music (and the lyrics) I'm listening to line up with my Christian faith and values?
- Does this song match up with my desire to live a life of integrity?
- Am I using my time wisely?
- What has control over me?

When you are being completely honest and seeking God's wisdom, these simple questions will help you make the right choices. They will help you intelligently choose what kind of music you will and will not invite into your mind.

Winning the Battle for Your Mind

Media can fool us. Never underestimate the incredible power of social media, music, movies, TV, videos, magazines, and the Internet. The direct influence they have on your mind can be concerning and overwhelming. The garbage in/garbage out principle is the strongest and most sensible principle for dealing with the media. If you feed your mind with negative influences, the negative *will* come out. If you feed it with positive messages, the positive will win. It's just that simple. What goes in must come out. Because your mind is so much a part of who you are and who you're becoming, let's look at a few practical suggestions for improving your thought life.

Program Your Mind to Think Good Thoughts

Here is a sentence for you to memorize: *I create change in my life when I gain control of my thoughts.* People who live truly satisfying lives are in the process of mastering their thought life. Listen to the apostle Paul's advice about your thought life:

> Whatever is true, whatever is noble, whatever is right, whatever is pure, whatever is lovely, whatever is admirable—if anything is excellent or praiseworthy—think about such things. Whatever you have learned or received or heard from me, or seen in me—put it into practice. And the God of peace will be with you.
>
> Philippians 4:8–9

Notice what Paul mentions as a result from thinking about good things—*peace.* When you plant good thoughts in your life, the roots will grow deep. When the seed of good thoughts begins to sprout, one of its many positive characteristics is peace.

Let me suggest a few ways to prepare yourself to think good thoughts: read and memorize Scripture, listen to good music, read inspiring books, and choose friends who will build you up. When you're praying, don't rush it. Remember, "As a man thinks in his heart, so is he."

A few years ago, when I needed to keep my focus on the Lord, I decided to read the entire New Testament. I divided it into ninety sections, approximately three chapters a day. On my calendar, I placed a big mark ninety days from the day I began. Reading the New Testament completely in a three-month period helped me discipline myself to read for ten to fifteen minutes a day, and it gave me the opportunity to plant good things in my life. Other people I know choose to read all one hundred fifty psalms and all thirty-one chapters of the book of Proverbs, every month. That's five psalms a day and one chapter of Proverbs.

If you really want to train your mind for good thoughts, set aside time each day to spend with God. Through the centuries, all the great men and women of God share one characteristic that stands out above the rest: *they all had a daily quiet time with God.* If you want to think good thoughts and keep your mind focused on God, you must "renew" your mind constantly with good input. Two Scripture verses have been especially helpful to me:

> You will keep in perfect peace all who trust in you, all whose thoughts are fixed on you!
>
> Isaiah 26:3 NLT

> Keep this Book of the Law always on your lips; meditate on it day and night, so that you may be careful to do everything written in it. Then you will be prosperous and successful.
>
> Joshua 1:8

God promises that if we focus our minds on Him, we will have peace and His perfect presence with us in everything we do. The hard work you put in to train and focus your mind on God will be worth it.

I know a woman who challenges the students she works with to go on what she calls a "starvation diet." This diet isn't about food but rather about starving your mind of media images that can weaken your mind against sexual integrity. She challenges her students to take on a thirty-day challenge to not watch or listen to anything that has sexually explicit words, images or even innuendos. After thirty days she asks the students if it helped them live out a life of sexual integrity. She says she has never met a student who tried this challenge and said it didn't help.

Now put the words "I can do all things through Christ who strengthens me" (Philippians 4:13 NKJV) into your mind. When you renew your mind, nothing is holding you back from becoming the person you were made to be. And with a renewed mind, you can live a life of sexual integrity.

DISCUSSION STARTERS

Think about your answers to the questions below and talk about them with an adult you trust.

1. What are the ways you've seen people put bad things in their minds?
2. How do you think poor choices about what to watch, listen to, or read can affect someone's quality of life?

3. In this chapter, there is a principle of starving your mind of poor choices. What would it look like to do that?

4. Read Romans 12:2. "Do not conform any longer to the pattern of this world, but be transformed by the renewing of your mind." What does it mean to you?

EIGHT

THE DANGERS OF PORNOGRAPHY

At age eleven, Taylor went online to check out baseball gloves at a sporting goods store. He innocently typed in the store's name, but he didn't find the store. Instead, he found pornography—countless images of men and women who were naked and, in some cases, performing sexual acts. Even though it was an accident, Taylor felt guilty and dirty. Soon, he found himself feeling drawn to look at the photos again, and over the next year and a half, he spent time each day looking at images like those. His hunger for more and even grosser photos and videos grew. Before long, Taylor was addicted to powerful images, always wanting more. By age thirteen he was starting to act out some of the crude behaviors he saw on the Internet.

Taylor wasn't a bad kid. He never meant to look at pornography in the first place and certainly didn't plan to get addicted. But he just kept giving in to the temptation to keep looking, and the addiction took over his life. Fortunately for Taylor, his parents finally realized something was going on. They checked the history on his computer, and they were shocked at what they saw. Together they were able to get some help from a therapist who specialized in pornography addictions. The therapist was able to show him how to put guardrails in place that would help him overcome this addiction. Today, Taylor is free from his pornography addiction, but he has to work at it every day. He would warn you to never start down that slippery road because it brought him so much confusion, shame, and heartache. It wasn't worth it. And honestly, I've never met a person who doesn't have regrets about their porn addiction. Like Taylor, it usually catches them by surprise.

When it comes to the human body and sexuality, we're all curious. And curiosity is normal and can be a good thing. Curiosity about our bodies and sex is part of the natural development that comes with puberty. That's why books like this one are written. And yet, curiosity without boundaries or guardrails can easily lead people into the trap of pornography. One bad decision can turn an innocent kid toward a destructive obsession that can have negative consequences for the rest of their life.

In the past, pornography was thought of as something that was only a struggle for guys. But in recent years, an increasing number of girls have admitted to looking at pornography as well. In today's digital age, pornography is surprisingly accessible, making it so anyone can stumble onto it without even trying. So, really any of us can be tempted to look at things that are harmful to our hearts, minds, eyes, and bodies. That's why guardrails and boundaries are so important!

Your Mind Takes a Picture

When you see a pornographic photo or video, your mind takes a picture of it, storing it inside your brain for the rest of your life. The more pornography you see, the more images that are stored in your mind—and you can bet it will affect your life.

I have successfully avoided most pornography over the course of my life. I think one of the reasons is because it wasn't as easy to access when I was growing up. When I was younger, pornography only existed in magazines or videos that had to be bought or rented from a store. Not many people would want to be seen walking into a store like that. But now, pornography is basically at your fingertips. Computers, mobile phones, YouTube, and almost every other streaming platform carry endless pornographic images and videos. In many ways, pornography is just harder to avoid now than it was when I was your age. But even still, when I was in eighth grade, I saw a picture of a woman with her top off in a *National Geographic* magazine, which of course is not a porn magazine. But that picture is still in my mind today. This shows the power of looking at images. Your mind remembers it.

If a person does not decide to live a life of sexual integrity, I don't know how it's even possible to keep yourself from viewing pornography. When I was a youth pastor, I was speaking to thirty thousand students at an international youth conference in New Orleans. That night in the Superdome where we had our conference sessions, we had an incredible time of worship with a well-known band and the best laser light show I have ever seen. I challenged the students to commit to sexual integrity. Remember, choosing a life and lifestyle of sexual integrity is much more than just not having sex before marriage. It's committing to sexual integrity, period. This includes not looking at pornography. That night, thousands of young people made the commitment. It was a cool experience.

Back at my hotel room, later that night, I was flipping through the channels on my television, and my eyes stopped on HBO. And there on my TV was full-frontal nudity with amazingly gross images, right on cable TV—no password required. I thought about all those high school students who were also in their hotel rooms all over the city and probably still up, watching TV. I wondered how many of them had seen those graphic sexual images as well.

The next day I did two workshops with four thousand students in each one. Since I was talking about healthy sexuality, it was only natural for me to ask the students how many had seen the HBO show the night before. I couldn't believe it—more than half of them raised their hands. I wonder if they changed the channel as quickly as I did. These students had made a decision to live with sexual integrity in the evening session and were immediately confronted with pornography just hours later.

When you think about your decision to live with sexual integrity, it must be viewed as a battle. And this battle will take self-control, discipline, accountability, and a strong faith to win.

The Porn-Addiction Progression

With any kind of addiction, most everyone assumes they'll be able to stop whenever they want. We all tend to think

we're invincible in that way. We think we can mess around with something without getting sucked in. But that's not how addiction works, and porn addiction is no different. In fact, many experts say the power of pornography is quite similar to crack cocaine or other drugs that hook people after the first few times. Porn addiction often starts out with a casual, almost innocent curiosity. A guy might check out a *Sports Illustrated* swimsuit issue or a *Victoria's Secret* catalog. Maybe a friend forwards a link to the website of a famous movie star who's not wearing a lot of clothes. But the addiction escalates to wanting to see total nudity because the other stuff gets boring. Then you'll want to see sexual acts, and eventually you're craving things that are more graphic and, honestly, just gross. The very nature of any addiction is that it escalates. Experts say there are five steps to pornography addiction.

1. Viewing Pornography

For most boys, their first exposure to pornography is on the Internet. For girls, it can be the Internet, reading about sexual experiences in a novel, or even chatting online. That first experience is often with a friend or at someone else's house, for example, while babysitting. Experts tell us that most young people today will view porn by accident on the Internet each month. Like I said before, porn is more available and easily accessible than any generation before you.

Unfortunately, you will see porn. And those images stick with you. The decision you'll have to make is: What will you do about it? Will you bounce your eyes? Will you linger and allow your mind to take a detailed picture? Or will you give into the temptation of allowing your eyes, mind, and heart

111

to take in the porn and hope it doesn't change you? *What you do with what you view will determine what happens next.* If you choose to live a life of sexual integrity, pornography will bother you, but you will be free to move on. If you don't, you could easily become addicted and enslaved to pornography, leaving you with some devastating results down the road.

2. Addiction

Did you know that the fastest-growing addiction in the world is pornography? It's enticing and exhilarating. You can easily find yourself coming back for more. Imagine your life filled with all kinds of experiences, but then it starts being taken over by your need to find time to look at pornography on a regular basis. Healthier experiences begin to fade away. You need the "high" of viewing porn, so you work your schedule around it. You feel shame and guilt, and you might even try to quit, but you're hooked, and you just keep coming back for more. You're not in control anymore because your addiction is controlling you.

At this stage, you need help—quick! The longer you stay addicted to anything, the harder it is to stop and the longer it takes to break free. I know good kids who innocently moved into an intense addiction to pornography and were too embarrassed to get help. They prayed, they struggled, but porn's hold was too much for them. They finally had to come clean, be humble, and admit they needed help. When it comes down to it, in its simplest form, addiction is your mind and body craving more. Believe me, there are people who understand how hard this is, and they want to help people just like you. Experts say that you typically can't overcome the chokehold of an addiction by yourself.

3. Escalation

As with most addictions, people eventually need a stronger or more intense high. For people addicted to pornography, they search for more hard-core graphic sites on the Internet. Or, while at one time they were disgusted with sexually direct messaging, now they find themselves participating in the very thing they thought was disgusting. As your addiction escalates, so does the frequency of the time you spend with porn. There are times when it overtakes you and becomes more important to you than anything else. A porn addict is like a drug addict who is desperate for a fix. The tragedy of escalation is that now the mind is being filled with even more graphic and immoral pictures. One young woman told me that her first time with pornography was when a friend showed her an Internet site with male models having sexual experiences. She said she was "grossed out." However, she was quickly drawn back to some of those sites, and then she moved rapidly from photos to videos to sexual conversations on social media. She told me she began to feel numb toward some of the images. At that point, she was already entering the next phase.

4. Desensitization

Desensitization is an extremely dangerous stage in the addiction process. The person has now seen enough graphic porn images that they are no longer excited by them. They are desperate for more thrills and willing to look at and do things that they never dreamed they would do before getting hooked. As a dad, I worry about the number of guys who have already gone down this road. I have three grown daughters who are beautiful, and when they were dating, we had our share of guys coming over to our house to spend time with them. I would wonder sometimes if any of them, many from Christian homes, had a secret obsession with porn.

If someone is in the desensitization stage, they are viewing people as sex objects. Men begin to view women as a sex object, not as a daughter of God who was created in the image of God and deserves to be treated with radical respect. And this can go both ways! Women can begin to view men as the means to get their physical and emotional needs met, rather than as someone created in God's image, deserving of radical respect. As mentioned in previous chapters, God created our sexuality, and He sees it as "very good." God-honoring sexuality is the goal, and if someone is in the desensitization phase of pornography addiction, they are far from having a wholesome view of sexuality. They are often just desperate to find greater thrills. The desensitization stage affects the way we view everyone and our relationships with others.

5. Acting Out Sexually

Although this could happen in an earlier stage as well, porn addicts will often make a jump from simply viewing photos and videos to fantasizing and even acting out what they've seen. A guest on my podcast who was addicted to porn said, "I would have never dreamed early on when I was dabbling in porn as a young person that as an adult, I would be driving down the street one day looking to hire a prostitute to try things that I thought were sick just a few months before. I lost my family. I lost my soul to porn."

The dangers of dabbling in pornography were also described to me by a very articulate sixteen-year-old who had

114

heard me speak at a conference. He said, "I would have never invited a stripper to come into my bedroom, yet going online for porn, I did it every night. Yet that was not enough for my cravings, so I went out and found the stripper. I was deeply disappointed and filled with shame, but I kept looking for that ultimate porn high." The young man was in for an uphill battle of reprogramming his mind and healing from his addiction. I hope you never get to this desperate place.

Almost daily I walk my dog at Dana Point Harbor, which is close to my home. I walk past people going to nearby meetings of Alcoholics Anonymous and Narcotics Anonymous. I am always so impressed by people who are working out their plans for sobriety. Completely staying away from drugs and alcohol is the only answer for an addict. They know they can't take a sip of alcohol or have even a small amount of drugs. For anyone who has dabbled in pornography (and even those who have not seen it!), the answer is the same: stay away from porn. It will only take you down a road you don't want to travel. No short-lived, feel-good experience is worth a lifetime of struggle.

The Internet and Porn

When I was young, most guys viewed pornography in *Playboy* magazines. However today, the availability and intensity of porn for both guys and girls is so much greater because of the Internet. As I've shared, even an occasional peek at porn can pollute your mind. Having sexual conversations and flirting online will also take you to places you don't want to be.

Let me tell you a story about a young woman named Lindsay. She was a good student who was active in sports and church. Through her social media account, she met a guy living in another state. In their online chats, she lied and said she was nineteen, even though she was much younger. The guy also said he was nineteen, though he was actually twenty-seven. Over time, their online relationship turned to sexual conversations, then very graphic video chats and long-distance phone calls.

Lindsay thought she was in love; she had never shared her feelings so freely with a guy. She decided to come clean and tell him how young she really was. He said that was all right because he liked younger girls. He still didn't tell her he was twenty-seven, though. Finally, they decided to meet. To make a long story short, she rode her bike to a nearby motel where they met in person for the first time and had sex. She loved the experience, and he flew back home.

Lindsay was still getting good grades, running cross-country, and active in church. At the same time, the relationship continued with the young man she thought was her dream come true. Then one day, he told her he had gotten another girl pregnant and was breaking up with Lindsay. She was devastated.

Lindsay managed to keep the guy a secret from everyone, but soon her depression was so bad that her mother took her to a counselor and psychiatrist. The psychiatrist prescribed an antidepressant. Finally, one night Lindsay was curled up in a ball crying her eyes out and told her mother the story. Her mom pulled the plug on Lindsay's computer and began the process of pressing charges against the adult who had abused her daughter.

One day Lindsay's mom and dad were going to church, but Lindsay said she didn't feel well and stayed home. When her mom and dad came home, they found Lindsay dead. She had been so overcome with sadness, guilt, and shame that she killed herself. That's why I'm so passionate about helping students like you make the wise choice to never get started in the first place.

Keep Committing to Sexual Integrity

I know Lindsay's story is horrific, but it shows what can happen when even good kids make terrible decisions. She wasn't able to recognize a sexual predator and understand what had happened. Not many people can.

But if you choose to live a life of sexual integrity, you won't ever find yourself in a devastating situation like that. Here are three quick ideas for staying free of pornography.

1. Run Away from It

The apostle Paul, when writing to the early church at Corinth said, "Flee from sexual immorality" (1 Corinthians 6:18). To *flee* means to take off running. When I was young, I was afraid of the dark. Okay, I'll admit it: there are times when dark places still creep me out! If I were ever in a dark place, I would start sprinting toward the light. That's what you should do if you see pornography. Run away from it as fast as you can. There is a story in the Bible about how the wife of a man whom Joseph worked for tried to tempt him. She took hold of his coat and said, "Come to bed with me." Do you know what he did? He ran away so fast, she was left standing there holding his coat.

117

Decide that you will keep your eyes away from porn. When you accidentally see porn in a message or on the Internet, delete it or move on without staring and tell a parent about it. When someone shows you a video with sexual images, leave the room. When you are watching a show or movie and a sexual image appears, find something else and don't look back. When you're reading a novel and suddenly find yourself reading about a steamy sexual experience, shut the book and get it out of your house! There is no value to you in reading that!

Also, don't share any personal information on the Internet and don't message with people you don't know. If you don't know a person in real life, you can't be friends online. If you were in a dark vacant alley, there is no way you would talk to a stranger, let alone flirt with them. But that's what people are doing online every day. Make the decision to never use the Internet in a sexual manner. You just might save your life!

2. Get Help Quickly

If you have seen too much pornography, get help now. Don't wait. You don't have to go through life carrying the weight of shame and guilt, always wondering if someone will find out. If you had a sickness and might possibly die, you'd probably go to the doctor and get the help you needed. The same is necessary for pornography. Porn damages our souls. Without help, you may never know the freedom of a beautiful relationship in marriage.

There are people near where you live who can help you through your problems and possible addiction. Believe me, they've heard worse stories than yours, and they are there to help. Don't put it off because of pride. You need to get help from someone you can sit and talk with to give you the right advice.[1]

3. Seek Accountability

When anyone talks to me about their problem with pornography, the first questions I ask are, "Do you have at least one accountability partner? (An accountability partner is a person with whom you are totally honest and who gives you wise advice.) Is there someone in your life you can tell when you've messed up?" If they answer yes, I encourage them to talk to that person. If they don't, I tell them I don't think they can battle any problem with pornography without accountability. I know it can be shameful, but there is power in sharing our struggles. I meet with four men every Tuesday morning. We all practice confession and accountability. Here is the principle direct from the Bible: "Therefore, confess your sins to each other and pray for each other so that you may be healed. The prayer of a righteous person is powerful and effective" (James 5:16). The principle is that when you confess your sins to a trusted person, there is healing. I am a better husband and father because of these accountability relationships. There are times I choose a healthier lifestyle just because I know I have to tell those friends what I'm doing.

So, no matter what your age, it is a great idea to find people you can absolutely trust, confess to, and share any problem you have. You want this person (or people) to be completely trustworthy. They should be the same sex as you, and they should be people who will pray for you, support you, and help you live by God's moral standards. That's what sexual integrity is all about.

DISCUSSION STARTERS

Think about your answers to the questions below and talk about them with an adult you trust.

1. What are some of the ways people see pornography in today's world?
2. What do you think are some of the dangers of experiencing pornography?
3. This chapter talked about a porn addiction progressing from viewing porn to acting out sexually. How do you think a porn addiction might change the way we look at the opposite sex or the way we view healthy sexuality?
4. How can a commitment to the Integrity Code help you to "turn your eyes from worthless things"?

NINE

RADICAL RESPECT: RELATING TO THE OPPOSITE SEX

Some of my friends who have known me for a long time would probably laugh at the idea that I would write a book about sex and our bodies. After all, I'm the guy who spilled an entire plate of spaghetti down the front of his shirt on his very first date. The plate landed upside down on my lap—and I was wearing white pants. I'm the guy who went to pick up a date on the wrong night in high school. Yep! I arrived at her door just as she was leaving with her boyfriend who was older and bigger than me. (Although, in my defense, I thought they had broken up.) Even my wonderful wife, Cathy, fell asleep on our first date on the way to dinner. Really!

Well, I may not have hundreds of dating success stories, but I do know that love, dating, and relating to the opposite sex are important parts of living a life of sexual integrity. I believe that how you relate to the opposite sex and how you engage with dating relationships will determine the success of your relationships. It also says a lot about what's important to you and whether you are trusting God for your future.

You may be thinking, *But I don't date yet.* That depends on what you consider dating to be. Many people think a date must be romantic and expensive. But dating happens any time you are relating to the opposite sex. Riding together in your parents' SUV with two guys and three girls could be considered a form of dating because guys and girls are relating. Walking home from school together is engaging with the opposite sex. Sure, it's not roses and a candle-lit meal, but anytime you are with someone of the opposite sex, you are relating and learning how to treat them. I think our culture puts way too much pressure on you to have romantic dates when there are many other ways of connecting.

Radical Respect

I love this concept of learning that the very best and right way to relate to the opposite sex, or anyone for that matter, is with *radical respect*. Culture does a horrible job of teaching us to radically respect each other. Remember from a previous chapter that we were all made by God and created in His image. This might be one of the most important concepts of living a life of sexual integrity. Culture says we need to think of ourselves, our wants, and our desires before anyone else. But as Jesus followers, we just can't do that! Every person we meet is made in the image of God and deserves to be honored and respected. We're called to put the needs of others above

our own. So, we can't take advantage of someone else just to meet our own emotional or physical needs. The apostle Paul summed up the Christian attitude when he said: "Do nothing out of selfish ambition or vain conceit. Rather, in humility value others above yourselves, not looking to your own interests but each of you to the interests of others. In your relationships with one another, have the same mindset as Christ Jesus" (Philippians 2:3–5). Your job is to consider another person's interest even above your own.

So, let me tell you about a couple I know. David and Donna are Christians. They like each other. David is dating Donna, a very cute girl who has a beautiful smile and a terrific personality. But because David is dating Donna, he's also (in a way) dating Jesus, who lives inside Donna. David is also a very special person. He is kind, good-looking, smart, and a great soccer player. But that's not all. David has Jesus Christ living inside him by the power of the Holy Spirit. This means Donna is, in a spiritual way, dating Jesus, who lives inside David. The bottom line is, *you should treat all people as if Jesus lives inside them.* We're called to radically respect all God's children. And if you really care about someone, then you want the very best for them.

This way of thinking and behaving is not just for people your age: it's also for older people like me. When I am around a woman, I can either treat her as a sister or I can treat her as a sexual object. Living with sexual integrity means that we guard our hearts, minds, bodies, and eyes from the bad and bounce them toward the good. Deciding to follow the way of radical respect is a great way to train yourself for sexual integrity, and it will help you avoid most of the problems you could have with the opposite sex.

123

So, decide *today* to relate to the opposite sex with radical respect. Start now, and as you begin a more serious approach to dating, radical respect will be a habit. Unfortunately, many of your friends will *not* choose to live with radical respect, so it might be tempting to think it doesn't really matter. But, if you choose to live a life of sexual integrity and demonstrate radical respect to the opposite sex, you will experience freedom and healthy relationships.

You may not be dating now, but most likely someday you will. So, here are a couple of other things to think about.

Caution: Exclusive Dating May Be Hazardous to Your Love Life.

There are two kinds of dating—*exclusive* and *inclusive*. Exclusive means it's just the two of you. It's steady, and it's serious. Inclusive means you are relating to many friends of the opposite sex by spending time together in groups. An inclusive date could be five girls and four guys who go to the mall together. It could be three guys and two girls who hang out at someone's house for pizza and a movie. Most of us have misunderstood dating. We think it must always be one-on-one. It doesn't have to be.

I knew a young couple we nicknamed "the clingers." Wherever they went, they were always clinging to each other. One was rarely seen without the other. When they finally broke up, neither of them had any good friends because they had spent all their time and energy with each other. Later both separately told me that they wished they had put energy into other friends as well. The "clinging" only to each other wasn't good for them on several levels. Here is some good advice: even if you do have a steady boyfriend or girlfriend, don't ignore other friendships. The sign of a healthy relationship is that there is not a desperate need for the other person to make you happy.

The Way You Approach Dating Will Say a Lot About Your Relationship with Jesus

Show me who you date and how you date, and I can tell you a lot about your faith and values. As a follower of Jesus, one of the most practical ways to practice your faith is in your dating life and relating to the opposite sex.

When it comes to dating, I'm always asked this question: "What's your opinion about Christians dating non-Christians?" It's a very important question to ask. Let me tell you why. First, Christians and non-Christians have a lot in common. And when we look at the life of Jesus, He often spent time with nonbelievers. So, in following His example, we should spend time with non-Christians too. But I don't think a Christian should be dating exclusively with someone who is not a Christian, even if it's not serious. The apostle Paul, who was a follower of Jesus and wrote many of the books in the New Testament in our Bible wrote this: "Do not be yoked together with unbelievers" (2 Corinthians 6:14). He was saying that believers should not marry unbelievers. It doesn't say anything about dating, but in a practical sense, dating is practice for marriage. And it's possible to start dating someone casually, thinking it doesn't matter what they believe, only to realize later that you're in love and you don't want to break up even though you don't share the same faith.

Does this mean you shouldn't have non-Christian friends? No. As I said before, Jesus often spent time with unbelievers. You might also be wondering if being a Christian means you won't be tempted to date someone who isn't a follower of Jesus. Not necessarily. If you are a Christian who is trusting Jesus to lead you, then you will have different values from someone who isn't trusting Jesus to lead them. Remember, it's just as easy to fall in love with a nonbeliever as with a believer.

I was speaking to a few thousand students one night about sexual integrity. After the talk, I took questions from the audience. One of the first questions was about Christians dating non-Christians, so I decided to give them a demonstration. I was standing on a stage. I asked the person to come up to the stage and reach their hand up to me from the floor. Then I asked if it was easier for me to pull them up onto the stage or for them to pull me off the stage onto the floor. As you can imagine, it was much easier for this student to pull me off the stage. (And they did!) My illustration was that it's almost always easier to be taken down than to be lifted up. I've got family members who have experienced that scenario. They dated and married non-believers who were nice people, but now neither follow Jesus.

Is It Love or Infatuation?

Did you know that the average person falls in love five times between the ages of thirteen and nineteen? So, you might have a huge crush on someone. You might even think you're in love. When I look back at my younger years, I was always falling in love with some girl. (I guess I've always been "above average!") For me it was:

Age 12 Chris
Age 13 Jeannie

Age 14 Nancy, then Geri (Geri was a girl!)

Age 15 Marla, back to Jeannie

Age 16 Carla and Carol (at the same time!)

Age 17 Carol

Age 18 Carol

Age 19 Cathy (this one lasted!)

As I look back now, I can see there was a huge difference between the love I had for Cathy and the infatuation I felt for Nancy. I liked Nancy, but after a few months we decided to go our separate ways. I knew I really loved Cathy because we still loved each other even through the hard times over a period of three years.

The difference between love and infatuation is long-term versus short-term. One day, Cathy and I took our daughters to the beach. I was people-watching—like usual. A group of young girls near us was very excited about one of the lifeguards. One girl loudly stated, "He's such a hunk! I'm in love, I'm in love!" So, naturally, I asked Cathy what she thought of the lifeguard. Even she said, "He really is very handsome." When the lifeguard slipped down from his tower and walked to the water, one of the young girls said, "I want to marry this guy. I've got to meet him." I laughed about the fact that she wanted to marry him before she'd even met him. I wanted to say, "Excuse me, but you're not in love; you're in infatuation."

The lifeguard story may seem a little extreme to you, but so many people make life-changing decisions in situations that are almost as silly. We get infatuation confused with true love. Here are some practical guidelines and questions to help you know if you're truly in love.

Do you like the other person? There is a difference between love and like. In some marriages, the people love each other but don't actually like each other. Those marriages are truly sad. It's possible to love someone without liking them, but don't settle for that in a relationship. God wants so much more for you!

Are you real and honest with each other? One sign of true love is that you can share your deepest doubts and dreams, disagree on some things, and still feel accepted.

Are you overly dependent? True love means you want the best for the other person and that you're not dependent on them to make you happy.

Is your love (or their love) self-centered? If it feels like they (or you) are always wondering "What's in it for me?" or if the love is selfish, it's not true love.

Is your love for Jesus as strong as your love for each other? A love that is tied together with the love of God is the strongest and best kind of love. If you can't answer yes to this question, then your relationship is a gamble.

Does your relationship bring you happiness and joy? I know several students who are currently staying in a relationship even though it is always adding stress and frustration to their lives. Truthfully, it's their low self-esteem that makes them want to stay in the relationship. I think that's an unwise reason to stay with someone.

Have you shared too much of your life too soon? I call this emotional or physical "streaking." Streaking is when someone is naked underneath a coat, and then at a certain time—like halftime at the football game—they take off the coat and streak, or run, naked in front of people. I think it's pretty gross, but it happens. In the same way, a lot of younger couples "emotionally streak" by sharing too much too quickly. This forces a couple to become too close emotionally, which will eventually lead them to becoming too close sexually.

Have both of you committed to sexual integrity? If the answer is no, then I would question the integrity of the relationship.

Love: 1 Corinthians 13–style

Here is a great definition of love. Love:

- is patient
- is kind
- is not jealous
- is not conceited (someone who is stuck on themselves)
- is not proud
- is not ill-mannered (someone who is rude and has bad manners)
- is not selfish
- is not irritable
- does not hold grudges
- is not happy with evil
- is happy with the truth

God is the only one who can love us perfectly. But this list can be a great measuring tool for your love relationship. Look at the previous list and think of someone you love or who loves you. Now write the words *rarely, sometimes,* or *almost always* next to the words that describe your relationship. It's a good exercise to see how the relationship is really going.

The information in this chapter is so important to your commitment to sexual integrity The way you view the opposite sex will play a big role in how you handle relationships. People who show radical respect don't have as many regrets about relationships. And the people who don't live with radical respect typically end up compromising their commitment to sexual integrity.

Susan decided she wanted to follow the Integrity Code, but she never really lived out the radical respect idea. Susan made a decision to live a life with sexual integrity, and her parents were very excited about that decision. She was active in school, active in her church youth group, and was one of the popular kids. Most of her friends didn't really care about sexual integrity. Susan eventually put her mind, body, eyes, and heart at risk. A few years later she started being noticed by guys, and she liked the attention.

At age seventeen Susan had mostly abandoned her view of radical respect. She became sexually active with a guy who was cute and popular but really wanted only one thing: sex. She gave her body as an act of love, and he gladly accepted it as an act of lust. Susan contracted a lifelong sexually transmitted disease, and the guy she thought was so great dropped out of her life completely. Today Susan is married and takes medicine for her STD. (Some call these STIs or sexually transmitted infections.) She also speaks to students like you and challenges them to not give their bodies to anyone outside of marriage. She knows firsthand the physical and emotional consequences. The better way to live is with radical respect.

DISCUSSION STARTERS

Think about your answers to the questions below and talk about them with an adult you trust.

1. Why do you think having radical respect for the opposite sex is difficult?

2. How can a negative dating relationship spoil your future and more serious relationships?

3. Read 1 Corinthians 13:4–9. Why does this seem like a very good standard of relating to the opposite sex?

4. How do you think the Integrity Code and the idea of radical respect go together?

TEN

THE POWERFUL INFLUENCE OF FRIENDS

The people you spend time with will play a huge part in determining the kind of person you are and who you'll become. Let me put it to you straight: *you will become like the people you hang around with*. This means that any of us will struggle to stick to a life of integrity if we are hanging out with the wrong kinds of friends. Someone once said, "What you tolerate in a friend, you eventually begin to imitate." Another once told me, "Show me who your friends are, and I will show you who you will become." This idea echoes a proverb I like: "Walk with the wise and become wise, associate with fools and get in trouble" (Proverbs 13:20 NLT). This is true with sexual integrity and life.

A Friendly Influence?

One of my favorite people from my days in student ministry was a guy named Norman. He wasn't blessed with beauty, brains, or bucks. Norman didn't have an easy childhood. His dad died when he was in elementary school, and even though his mother was wonderful, she wasn't home much because she worked long hours to pay the bills. No one would ever say that Norman was handsome. In fact, Norman looked like the quintessential nerd.

What made Norman unique was that he changed friends and fads as often as some people changed clothes. I met Norman when he was entering middle school, and in the few years I knew him, Norman was a:

- surfer
- punk rocker
- football team manager
- cross-country runner
- drummer in a rock band
- cowboy (and that's difficult in Newport Beach, California)
- high school band member
- drama club member
- skateboarder
- student body officer
- student leader at church
- heavy drinker
- heavily involved with pornography

Norman moved quickly from one crowd to another. I never knew what Norman would become next. He was like a chameleon (you know, the lizard that changes colors to match its surroundings). Every time Norman changed friends, he became, in essence, a different person. His new "friends" had a significant influence on who he was at that moment. As you can imagine, this wasn't always a good thing.

Norman had a poor image of himself. One day he confided in me, "I don't really like the *real* Norman, so I'm trying to become someone I can respect. I think if I were accepted by a group of people who liked me, I'd be okay." That was a deep statement for a guy like Norman. In his own way, he was beginning to understand that because he didn't like himself, he was trying to be somebody else. He was also beginning to understand that whomever you spend time with has a big influence on who you become. We'll come back to Norman later in the chapter.

Choose Your Friends Wisely

Some people never really think about how much influence their friends have on their lives. Because friends do make such a difference, it's so important to choose your friends wisely. Let's take a friendship inventory:

1. Do your friends bring you up or pull you down?
2. What do you like and dislike about your friendships?
3. What can you do to make sure you have friends who influence you in a positive way?
4. Do you have friends who help you stick to a life of sexual integrity or pull you away from it?

When I was a junior in high school, I became a Christian. I realized that the friends I had spent most of my time with were not the best influence in my life. One of the wisest decisions I ever made was choosing a new group of friends that year. It was a tough decision, but looking back, it was the *right* decision. When I went back for my ten-year high school reunion, it was so clear to me just how important that decision had been in my life. Ten years later, my previous friends were struggling with drugs, divorce, and failure. My newer friends were much more together—and happier.

This kind of decision is extremely hard. And if your need for love and acceptance from others is out of balance because of a low self-image, it will be even tougher. It's also true that the decisions you make today will affect you for the rest of your life. Please don't ever underestimate the influence of your friends. Choose them wisely. They may influence you forever, including your choices connected with sexual integrity.

Peer Pressure

You and I have an incredibly strong need to be loved and accepted by our friends and family. The drive to be liked is so strong that we'll do almost anything to be accepted by our peers. Peer pressure will be one of the driving forces behind the most difficult struggles in your life.

What kind of power causes sixteen-year-old Janet to have sex when it goes against the way she was brought up and she knows better? What power causes Tom at age fourteen to drink a six-pack of beer with some new "friends," steal his family's car, and go for a joyride? He didn't like the guys he was drinking with or the taste of alcohol. And he was scared to death he would get caught with the car. Krista, age thirteen, felt so much pressure by her friends to "identify" as a lesbian even though she wasn't a lesbian. But she couldn't fight it and even acted out what she didn't really believe was her sexual identity. What power, what pressure causes people to do things they really don't want to do? Peer pressure.

Janet went to a new school. She wanted to be in the most popular group, but she wasn't. She didn't like her looks. When she compared herself to the people around her, she felt like she never measured up. She started to hang around with a group that was more adventurous and riskier than she was used to and went to one of their parties. Janet got drunk, but she didn't realize how drunk. After a few more drinks, she was not in control of her emotions, and her decision-making process was blurred. A guy she really liked came up to her and started flirting. They started kissing, and he convinced her to go with him to a bedroom. Janet wanted this guy to like her so much that she allowed him to have sex with her. It was her first time, and Janet got pregnant.

Tom wanted to be accepted by a group of neighborhood guys who were a few years older. He didn't want to be known as the "perfect" Christian kid. He drank too much, took his parents' car, and with his "friends" in the car, crashed the car in downtown San Clemente, California. Fortunately, even though the car was totaled, no one was critically injured. This time they were lucky.

Krista experimented sexually with other girls, even though she knew in her heart it wasn't who she really was. She later told me in tears, "I just wanted to feel accepted by my group of friends."

Make no mistake about it, peer pressure is extremely powerful. The pressure to belong and be accepted will push you to make some very poor decisions.

The apostle Paul summarized some of his deepest feelings with these words:

> I don't understand myself at all, for I really want to do what is right, but I can't. I do what I don't want to—what I hate. I know perfectly well that what I am doing is wrong, and my bad conscience proves that I agree with these laws I am breaking. But I can't help myself, because I'm no longer doing it. It is sin inside me that is stronger than I am that makes me do these evil things.
>
> I know I am rotten through and through so far as my old sinful nature is concerned. No matter which way I turn I can't make myself do right. I want to but I can't. When I want to do good, I don't; and when I try not to do wrong, I do it anyway. Now if I am doing what I don't want to, it is plain where the trouble is: sin still has me in its evil grasp.
>
> It seems to be a fact of life that when I want to do what is right, I inevitably do what is wrong. I love to do God's will so far as my new nature is concerned; but there is something else deep within me, in my lower nature, that is at war with my mind and wins the fight and makes me a slave to the sin that is still within me. In my mind I want to be God's willing servant but instead I find myself still enslaved to sin.
>
> So you see how it is: my new life tells me to do right, but the old nature that is still inside me loves to sin. Oh, what a terrible predicament I'm in! Who will free me from my slavery to this deadly lower nature? Thank God! It has been done by Jesus Christ our Lord. He has set me free.
>
> Romans 7:15–25 TLB

I'm not sure about you, but I can easily identify with what Paul wrote in Romans. There is a battle inside all of us. The battle against peer pressure is one you'll fight for the rest of your life. It's always going to be difficult to resist the temptation to make choices just to get someone else's approval. Adults struggle with peer pressure every day. Unfortunately, it's not something you'll grow out of as you get older. However, as you discover how to keep your self-esteem rooted in God's love, you can win this battle. Just because you'll have to face peer pressure the rest of your life doesn't mean you have to give into it. Negative peer influence is something you can—and must—defeat.

Even though you may not want to hear the truth, here it is: If your closest friends experiment with drugs, the odds are very strong that you will also. If your friends are sexually active, you will most likely become sexually active too. If your closest friends look at porn, so will you. We become like the people we hang around.

A fourteen-year-old guy once asked me, "What's so important about my friends anyway?" "You tell me," I replied. After thinking about it for a while, he took out a piece of paper and wrote the following thoughts:

My friends influence

- what I think about myself
- what language I use
- what I think of my parents
- what I wear
- what's "in" and what's not
- what I think about my teachers

- how I act
- what parties I attend
- whether studying is important
- whether or not to drink or vape
- what is right or wrong
- whether to have team spirit
- whether I should keep going to church
- how I should spend my money
- what I want to do when I graduate from high school

When he shared his thoughts with me, I looked at him and said, "I think you answered your own question."

Now, let me ask you a question. Do your friends build you up and help you live out a deeper faith with integrity, or do they hold you back and move you in a negative direction? Only you can answer that question honestly in your heart. But don't underestimate the influence of your friends and peer pressure.

Make Positive, Healthy Friendships a Priority in Your Life

As you know, there is negative peer pressure, but positive peer influence is just as powerful. Friendship is a priceless gift from God. There are few things in life that are as important or as wonderful as true friendship. A good friend is a greater gift than almost anything else in life. So, is making positive, healthy friendships a priority in your life? Think for a moment about the three people who are your closest friends. Now take a few minutes to list why you consider them true friends.

Here's a simple but important formula. If you want true friends, then you must be a true friend. Let's consider some qualities of a true friend. A true friend is:

1. *Caring and available.* Nothing is more important than the gift of your time and genuine concern.
2. *Encouraging.* When you affirm and support your friends, you are building their self-esteem by *showing* them they are important and that you believe in them.
3. *Willing to sacrifice.* A true friend goes the extra mile and can be counted on, even when it's not convenient.
4. *Patient.* No one is perfect, but a true friend sticks around even when things get hard.
5. *A good listener.* Listening is the language of love.
6. *Loyal.* The Bible says, "If you love someone you will be loyal to him no matter what the cost" (1 Corinthians 13:7 TLB).
7. *Truthful.* A true friend tells you the truth in love, even if it hurts.

Now, as you look over this list and think about your friends, how do they measure up? How do you measure up? If you need work in one or more of these areas, now is the time to start.

Christian Friends Will Usually Encourage You to Move Closer to God

I promised you I would get back to the story of my "nerd" friend Norman. Sometime later in Norman's high school

141

years, he started getting much more serious about his relationship with Jesus and the church youth group. At church, he found a crowd of people who came from different groups at school, but they all seemed to get along well at church. He found friends in the church who genuinely liked him for who he was. They didn't try to turn him into someone else. As Norman became more comfortable with his new friends, he began to open up about his hurts and past mistakes. They accepted him, and he felt loved. He experienced God's love through the unconditional love of his friends.

It took Norman a long time to believe he belonged. He was learning to understand that his identity was rooted in the love of Jesus and the acceptance of positive friendships. These friends encouraged him to live a life of sexual integrity, not because it was a bunch of rules but because it was the best way to follow God's will. His Christian friends *showed* him that God was real, and that reality changed his life. Today, Norman is well on his way to becoming one of the most successful youth pastors I know. Sure, there is negative peer pressure, but don't underestimate the power of positive peer influence! Positive friendships will help you become all that God created you to be. So, go for it!

DISCUSSION STARTERS

Think about your answers to the questions below and talk about them with an adult you trust.

1. How can negative peer pressure influence someone to abandon their faith and values?

2. Positive peer influence is just as powerful as negative peer pressure. How can friends help you follow the Integrity Code?

3. Who are the good friends in your life who influence you in a positive way? What are some ways they've influenced you?

4. What can you do to become a better friend to others? Where can you find more friends who will help you stick to the Integrity Code?

ELEVEN

FLIRTING, MODESTY, AND HOW FAR IS TOO FAR?

While writing this chapter, my family went to a wonderful resort in Ixtapa, Mexico. As a natural-born people-watcher, hanging out at the beach while writing about sexual integrity is . . . well, interesting. Let's just say this week I have seen it all.

One young teenage girl was walking in the crowded market wearing a shirt that simply read FLIRT. It had to be two sizes too small, and the word *FLIRT* drew attention to her chest. As I watched the scene, it was obvious that men, young and old, were staring at the girl's top. It was actually kind of gross and made me feel uncomfortable that even older guys were looking at her. When she turned around, I saw that the same word was printed across the back of her very tight short shorts. I guess she chose her clothes to fit a theme! Now, here's the deal: whether she was aware of all the stares and sexual thoughts being sent her way, the fact remains that what we wear and how we act plays an important part in living out a life of sexual integrity.

I'm not super prude, I promise. And it's not just the clothes we wear at the beach or lake. We used to host an FCA (Fellowship of Christian Athletes) meeting in our home. Three female volleyball players were sitting at the meeting with about four inches of BC showing. ("BC" stands for butt crack in our family.) Every guy at this meeting took a double take. I don't believe the girls were doing this on purpose. I just think it didn't cross their minds that the guys were trying to see as much skin as possible.

This chapter is not just for girls. Sure, guys tend to look at skin and body parts more than girls, but guys can be just as irresponsible with flirting, modesty, and creating healthy boundaries as girls.

A mom friend of mine once told me that when it comes to developing personal, healthy boundaries, we must guard our bodies against the "weak links of compromising clothes, compromising company, and compromising actions." I couldn't agree more. One of the battles most students end up having with their parents is over those three issues. I know my wife and I had some battles with all three of our daughters. So, let's look at these challenging issues through the grid of sexual integrity.

Compromising Clothes

When I was in sixth grade, I bought a pair of blue tennis shoes with my own money. My dad was not okay with blue tennis shoes! He had only seen white and black, and

146

he thought if black or white shoes were good enough for him, they were good enough for me. Believe it or not, tennis shoes in different colors had just become popular. (Okay, now you can really tell I'm an old guy.) Years later when I reminded my dad of that story, he'd laugh and deny it. He had become a cool grandpa who wore skater shoes of all different colors! My dad was wrong back then when he fought with me about the shoes. Blue tennis shoes were probably not a battle worth fighting. However, today some clothing issues are a problem. Let me speak to you for a moment as a dad.

Girls, guys look at skin. So, if you are showing skin, guys are checking you out. My daughter Rebecca is beautiful. When she was in eighth grade, she went to church one day in clothes that were a bit too revealing. She didn't look trashy, but I decided to use it as a learning lesson. "Rebecca," I said, "I hope you enjoy wearing this outfit today because it is the last time you will wear it. I can see your underwear and bra. Guys look at stuff like that." I had hoped her response would be, "Thanks for your input, Dad. I really appreciate it, and I'll change clothes immediately. You're the best!" Instead, she responded with something more like a disgusted look and the words, "Dad, you are so old-fashioned. Guys don't notice. Plus, *everybody* wears outfits like this!"

Later that day, Rebecca and I went out for frozen yogurt and then shopped for a more appropriate outfit. Basically, I bought the old outfit from her and bought her a new one too. I realized this lesson was going to cost me, but I figured it was worth it. During the time we were hanging out and eating yogurt, I mentioned to her that *men tend to have a weakness for looking at women's bodies.* She again told me

I was gross, and she didn't agree. I challenged her to ask her guy friends. Later I found out they all agreed with me!

I wasn't asking Rebecca to dress like a grandma, and I'm not suggesting you should either. I just want girls and guys to rethink what they have in their closet and choose clothes they like that also honor a commitment to integrity. I am absolutely convinced that you can wear cool and appropriate clothing without having to compromise your commitment to style.

If you show a lot of skin or wear tight clothes, you need to ask the question, "Am I trying to get the attention and desire of guys?" One person I know says that we should consider who our fashion role models are and if they help us honor God with the Integrity Code.

Compromising Company

We've already talked about how friendships play a big part in who you are and who you'll become. If you hang out with kids who flirt and talk about sex a lot, then you're entering the slippery slope of sexual compromise before you even get started.

When I was in junior high, I hung out with a guy who would describe in detail what he would like to do with girls. He had a dirty joke for every occasion. Sometimes I was grossed out by what he said. But I must admit, my curiosity would often get the best of me, and I would come back for more. Eventually (this was before I knew anything about sexual integrity), I began to change some of my behavior to fit in with him. Thankfully, he moved away, and I switched friends, or I might have found myself in trouble.

The Bible has a great insight: "Bad company corrupts good character" (1 Corinthians 15:33). The point is clear: If your friends dress a certain way, you'll probably end up dressing that way too. If your friends act in a certain way, you'll probably follow. I know one girl who had to quit watching rom-coms and reading romance novels. She told me all her friends were into that kind of stuff, and she almost felt like she was addicted. Moving away from compromising things and possibly even certain friendships may be the best decision she could make for her integrity.

Compromising Actions

I hope there are lots of other voices in your life warning you about the things that can lead you to compromise your integrity. However, as a dad, I want to mention a few more things that can get in the way of the life of sexual integrity we've been talking about.

Guys flirt with their hands, emotions, and words. When guys have their hands all over a girl, even if it looks like they are teasing, it is flirting. When guys talk about sexual things in a teasing way, they are flirting. If a guy is playing with a girl's emotions, he is most likely flirting. I flirt with my wife, and she flirts with me. That's natural and good. But when people flirt for the wrong reasons, it is very possible that it can lead to compromising and even dangerous situations. One girl told me about the time she innocently started rubbing the back of a guy she had met at camp. He then asked if he could return the favor, but as she said, it quickly turned into "more than a back rub, with his hands moving to some very private parts." She said it caught her off guard, and she had no idea what to say or do. So, she didn't do anything and just let him do what he wanted. She should have said "Stop!" but she also shouldn't have put herself in that situation.

Okay, it's time to add things to the "don't go there" list of compromising actions, some not-so-obvious things like the tickle fight, massage, and even some forms of hugs. I'm not trying to be over-the-top. I just know that playful touching is not as innocent as some would think. For example, when guys go to their first middle school dance, many of them are trying to choose who they want to dance with, in hopes of getting a chance to press against their breasts. Sorry if this offends you, but it's true.

Part of growing up is relating to the opposite sex. Don't get me wrong; I love the fact that girls and guys can have fun together. It's just that certain actions won't help us follow our Integrity Code. And just because something may not feel like a big deal to you doesn't mean it's not a big deal to someone else.

My friend Jill told me that when she was dating her (now) husband, they would periodically take naps next to each other. I said, "I bet that tempted John." She laughed at me and said, "Absolutely not." I said, "Ask your husband." The next day she came back to me and sheepishly said, "You were right. John told me it was very tempting and difficult for him."

So, this is why your parents will probably put limits on your alone time with the opposite sex and insist on keeping the door open in all rooms you are in together. They will probably challenge you to not go to the wrong place at the wrong time with the opposite sex. They will challenge you to not talk about sex with your boyfriend or girlfriend. Again, not because sex is bad or wrong, but because the temptations are strong at any age.

Creating Safe Boundaries

As you grow and develop through the teen years and beyond, one of the keys to living with sexual integrity is creating safe and healthy boundaries with your life. Personally, I use what I call the Ephesians 5:3 test, which says, "But among you there must not be even a hint of sexual immorality, or of any kind of impurity, or of greed, because these are improper for God's holy people." Basically, this test keeps me honest about my motives and helps me be more intentional about creating safe boundaries.

Here are four especially important boundaries or limits to keep working on and following to live a life of sexual integrity.

1. Keep Your Eyes Free of Sexual Sights (sites)

   The Bible talks about your eyes as the "lamp of your body" (Luke 11:34). As we have talked about before, it's impossible to avoid seeing sexual things, but the important and most impactful thing is what you do when you view it: bounce your eyes, turn your head, turn off the computer, change the channel, or excuse yourself from the movie. This takes major discipline. But first it requires deciding to do it. Nobody said it would be easy, but it is the right thing to do.

   Paul gave Timothy some great advice, "Train yourself to be godly." (I mentioned this Scripture in chapter 7.) In today's sex-obsessed world, it will take discipline and God's strength to keep you free from the garbage that will come your way. Don't underestimate the power of lust: it starts with our eyes and moves to our minds; then it reaches into our hearts and is sometimes acted out with our bodies. All four of those areas of your life are tied to your soul and a commitment to the God.

2. Set Standards Now

If you want to live with sexual integrity, you will have to "pre-decide" what your sex limits will be. When I spoke to my youth group about sex, the question students asked most often was, "How far is too far?" That's the wrong question to be asking. It's not how far can you go, but how far *should* you go?

Now is the best time to write out and commit to a plan for sexual integrity. Don't wait until you're dating. Sometimes it's too late. If you think you'll make a good decision in the moment, there is a good chance you won't. If you wait until you're feeling tempted to go too far physically with someone, your feelings will probably push you to keep going farther than you meant to. Create the plan before you ever have a relationship. Talk about the plan with your parents if possible, or someone else you trust from your church or school. Then, when you have the plan in place, you can ask them to help you keep focused with your plan for sexual integrity.

3. Commit to an Alcohol- and Drug-Free Lifestyle

You may be wondering why I would suggest this lifestyle boundary in a book on sexual integrity. Let me tell you about Julia. At age fifteen she had never had a sip of alcohol. Her friends and priorities had been slipping since middle school, but she had stayed strong with her commitment to stay away from alcohol. However, now she was running with a different crowd. Most of them did drink, and she had been to a few parties where there was drinking, but she still didn't have any. Enter Robert. Robert was seventeen, a star football player, and in Julia's words, "a hunk." She met him at a party, and he seemed to be interested in her. Robert had a beer in his hand, and she could tell it wasn't the only beer he had drunk that night. He offered her a drink. She didn't want to make it awkward, so she drank it. No big deal, she thought. He handed her another. She wasn't sure how many beers she drank, but when we later talked, it wasn't the beer she worried about. She was worried that she had possibly had sex with Robert. She had apparently passed out, and when she woke up, her underwear was not where it should have been. She was so scared, wondering how she could have had sex with someone and not even remembered it. Fortunately for Julia, she wasn't pregnant, but how sad to think that her first sexual experience happened while she was passed out and with a guy who totally took advantage of her.

Here's the deal. When you drink or take drugs, you lose control of your judgment and ability to make good decisions. Far too many young people end up breaking their commitment to integrity because they were literally not in their right mind. Not all stories are as bad as Julia's, but you might be surprised by how many students say they broke their integrity code because of being drunk or high. A recent study reported that "as many as 70 percent of college students admit to having engaged in sexual activity, primarily as a result of being under the influence of alcohol, or to having sex they wouldn't have had if they had been sober."[1] Now *that* is a remarkable finding about the power of being under the influence of a mind-altering drug like alcohol. Besides it being against the law for you to drink or use drugs, it can take you to a place you really don't want to go.

4. Don't Flirt With "Technical Virginity"

This is the section I wish I didn't have to write. If you were older, I would be even more direct and graphic. There is a growing trend with preteens and young teens to engage in oral sex. When my youngest daughter was ten, this subject was in the news a lot because a former president had engaged in oral sex with a White House intern. He point-blank said that oral sex is not sex. He may have been a brilliant person, but he was wrong on this point. My daughter heard all the talk on the news and innocently asked, "Daddy, what is oral sex?" In case you haven't figured it out yet, I feel pretty comfortable talking about this subject. But having my ten-year-old daughter ask me that question was almost too much! In the most discreet way I could, I explained that oral sex was when someone puts their mouth on another person's genitals. Of course, she thought it was gross. However, the number of kids in late elementary and middle school who are already participating in oral sex is frightening. A large percentage of girls who do this still consider themselves virgins— "technical virgins." Another term for some of these same kids is "friends with benefits." Believe me, having a sexual relationship with a "friend" is incredibly complicated and definitely not casual.

Today's experts on sexuality have a different definition than some students. If you think I'm blunt, you should meet my friend, Pam. Here is what Pam says about the issue of being a technical virgin: "The medical line that defines sex is this: Any genital contact at all, hand to genital, mouth to genital, or genital to genital, is sex." She adds, "If you have had genital contact at all, you have had sex."[2]

Too many young people today think they are living a life of sexual integrity if they do everything but have intercourse. I disagree. Often "everything but" leads to "everything gone." Not only do most people agree that oral sex is more intimate than genital to genital sex, but oral sex often leads to intercourse.

The time to make decisions about all this is now. Choose to live with sexual integrity and be willing to go against the grain of the culture. I have a T-shirt that says, "No Regrets." Make that a theme for your life as well.

DISCUSSION STARTERS

Think about your answers to the questions below and talk about them with an adult you trust.

1. What parts of this chapter did you disagree with? What were the parts you agreed with?

2. Why do you think I chose the word *compromise* when I talked about clothing, company (friendships), and actions?

3. What would it look like for you to wear things you like while also being modest? What do you think makes that so challenging?

4. Creating safe boundaries was a theme in this chapter. What are some safe boundaries that could help you?

TWELVE

SEXUAL ABUSE

I hope you never have to experience the trauma and heartbreak of sexual abuse. It is one of the worst tragedies in our world. If you have been sexually abused, I wrote this chapter for you. And if you haven't, I hope you'll read it anyway so you can be helpful if you ever know someone who has. Unfortunately, a large percentage of people do experience sexual abuse, and this is an especially important chapter to read to help you understand the traumatic effects of sexual abuse and how to prevent it from happening to you.

When you were younger, your parents needed to teach you to look both ways when crossing streets and not to talk to strangers. It's just as important to learn how to prevent sexual abuse. Some of these safeguards may not come naturally, but you can and should make them a part of your life.

I will talk more about it at the end of the chapter, but make sure you understand that *no one has the right to make you feel uncomfortable by a touch or word. You have the right to say no to anyone or anything that makes you feel uncomfortable, or awkward, or doesn't fit within your Integrity*

Code. Unfortunately, the world is filled with people who have the wrong view of their sexuality and life. And sometimes those are people we know and love. If for any reason you find yourself in a difficult situation, immediately talk with your parents or an adult you really trust. It's so important that you get help with getting out of the situation and with processing your thoughts and feelings about what happened. The sooner you can do that, the better off you will be.

I wish you could have been with me at lunch today. I sat with one of the most outstanding men in our community. He's rich, incredibly handsome, and one of the funniest people I know. To be honest, if I start comparing my life to his, I always lose.

Today was different. He told me about his childhood. Tears were flowing from his eyes as he shared one of the worst sexual abuse stories I have ever heard. He has always looked like he's got it all together, but on the inside, this man was falling apart in every way. He had been a victim of one of the worst crimes imaginable. His grandfather, a man he had loved and trusted, had sexually molested him regularly from ages eleven to sixteen. My friend had never told anyone, including his wife. He had buried his hurt and pain, but now, because he had never gotten help to deal with what had happened, memories of those experiences and feelings were coming to the surface in a way that was torturing him.

This is a serious chapter. There is nothing funny about sexual abuse. Nobody likes to talk about it, and nobody really wants to hear about it. But the cold, hard, frightening facts tell us that sexual abuse affects the lives of millions of people. And they often just wish it would go away.

Although the statistics vary, about one out of three young women will be sexually abused by the age of eighteen.

One out of six young men will be sexually abused by age eighteen.

The real statistics are likely higher than this. The latest findings suggest the problem could be far more widespread.

Sexual Abuse Is Real, and It's Everywhere

If you have been a victim of sexual abuse, you might not have ever read any books about it. But every part of your life is clouded by the fact that something very horrible has happened to you. And if you, personally, have never been sexually abused, someone you care about probably has.

From my counseling experience, I knew that sexual abuse was a problem. I had no idea, though, just how common it was until I started speaking about the subject. Wherever I go, when the subject is brought up, people who are devastated by their experience come to me and want to talk.

Let me introduce you to some special people who were in my youth group when I was a youth pastor. They looked and acted like everyone else, but inside they were keeping a terrible secret that was tearing them apart. All the names and some of the situations have been changed for reasons of confidentiality, but these stories are real.

Emily was babysitting at her ex-boyfriend Tom's house. She was very close to his little sister and his family, even though she and Tom had broken up. Tom's stepfather had always been nice to Emily. In fact, she often wished that her dad were more like Tom's stepfather. Tom's family was going out to dinner and a play while Emily watched the youngest child. The stepfather, Ted, would be home, but he would be working in a back room.

159

As soon as Emily put the little girl to bed, Ted came into the kitchen and asked Emily if she wanted some popcorn. Emily loved popcorn. She said, "Thanks. That will go good with what I'm watching on television."

Ted made the popcorn, then sat down on the couch next to Emily and started watching with her. Emily complained that her back was sore after playing softball. So, Tom's stepfather began to massage her back. At first, he rubbed outside her sweater, but after a while he moved his hands under her sweater.

Emily froze. She didn't know what to do. She didn't know if this "nice" man was going to go further or was just doing her an innocent favor. Emily was tense and nervous. In a soft voice, Tom's stepfather told her to relax; it would be better for her backache. Eventually, Ted began feeling her breasts. The phone rang. Emily was grateful for the distraction. Tom's stepfather—reluctantly, it seemed—got up to answer his phone. Emily had been sexually abused.

When Monica was nine years old, her fourteen-year-old brother molested her. It was a terrible, traumatic experience. She didn't tell anyone, because her brother threatened to kill her if she did. The next month, her brother raped her. For the next two and a half years, he had sex with her, always vowing to kill her if she told anyone.

Monica never told a soul. Her brother was a violent person, and she feared for her life. She pulled away from people and activities she enjoyed. She failed most of her classes and experimented with drugs given to her by her brother. Finally, years later, her brother was arrested for armed robbery, and Monica felt free of the horror of these traumatic experiences.

An acquaintance of Monica invited her to a weekend retreat at a Christian camp. There, for the first time in her life, Monica heard about God's unconditional love for her through Jesus Christ. She wanted to become a Christian, but her past experiences haunted her and kept her from accepting Christ. After coming home from camp, she made an appointment with a female youth pastor and told her story. Monica had been sexually abused.

Steve was seven when a babysitter molested him.

Daniel's favorite uncle molested him on a camping trip and confused Daniel by telling him that all uncles do this with their favorite nephews.

Older boys in the neighborhood sexually abused Emma. When she told her parents, her mother didn't believe her. Emma's father laughed.

All these people were sexually abused.

The stories go on and on. Just in the past few months, I have heard horror stories of a man videotaping a young girl in the shower, older males exposing themselves to innocent children, a date rape, adults sharing pornographic photos with children, and other stories I can't put into writing. Sexual abuse is real, and it's everywhere. I'm so sorry to have to even bring up these stories, but they are real, and they affect people on multiple levels. Sexual abuse is too widespread not to talk with you about it.

Good News for Victims of Abuse

Unfortunately, most people who have been sexually abused in one way or another keep their pain and experiences to themselves. Sometimes they feel ashamed, thinking that it's somehow their fault. Or they think if they can just forget about it, it might just go away. But that's not how it works. It doesn't go away—*ever.* I would even say that without help, a person who has been sexually abused can never have a healthy self-image or a life free from the pain of their past.

But there is good news for those who struggle in this area. Thousands of people who have been sexually abused have received help. They have experienced hope and healing! If you are a victim of sexual abuse—or any kind of abuse—you are not alone. People all around you suffer with the same issues. And they are probably dealing with their hurt in a similar way.

Here are four things I want to say to anyone who has been sexually abused:

1. It's not your fault.
2. Get help. Don't suffer in silence.
3. There is hope.
4. God cares. He really does.

It's Not Your Fault

Sexual abuse is always the fault of the abuser. Sadly, most victims blame themselves for what happened to them. But it is not their fault! It's time to put the blame in the proper place. If someone robbed you and stole your money, or if a drunk driver hit you, would you blame yourself? Of course not! When you have been sexually abused in any way, you have become a victim of a horrible crime. The abuser is sick. *It's not your fault.*

Get Help; Don't Suffer in Silence

The first step toward recovery is to get help. Sometimes it's embarrassing. You might feel like you don't want to reveal a deep, dark family secret. But you will not get better if you don't get help. If you choose to suffer in silence, you are choosing to get worse. You can't wish away your hurt. There are licensed counselors and therapists who are incredibly good at helping countless people heal from the pain of being sexually abused.

Isabella told her youth pastor that six months earlier, she had been at a party where an older guy forced her to have sexual intercourse with him. Isabella said she felt "cheap and used," but she was afraid to tell anyone. She was even more afraid that if she did tell someone, it would get back to the guy who abused her.

Her youth pastor did what the law required him to do and reported the rape. As the story unfolded, it was revealed that at least fifteen other girls had also been sexually abused by this one young man. Isabella received excellent support from a counselor who helped her. She worked through her thoughts and feelings about what had happened, and she has experienced emotional healing. Isbella's progress has been remarkably fast. If she had waited longer to get help, she may well have developed destructive behavioral patterns that would have taken years to undo. If you have been sexually abused, getting help can keep you from living in a constant state of anxiety, crisis, and chaos. Please don't suffer alone.

I urge people who have been sexually abused not to wait another day, but to reach out for help immediately. If you have been sexually abused and have never told anyone, then you are

163

reading this chapter for a reason. I believe God wants you to get the help you need, so tell your story to an adult you trust.

There Is Hope!

If you have been hurt and hurt deeply, then it may be difficult for you to imagine that life will ever be better. But thousands before you have been set free from the pain after they got help.

When Sarah was fourteen, her stepfather abused her in every way. Sarah told no one and acted as if nothing had happened. Her schoolwork did not suffer; it even improved. No one knew her inner pain, until one day she took a bottle of her mother's prescription sleeping pills. She prayed she would die. When Sarah woke up, she was in the hospital.

A good psychiatrist asked her if she would be willing to talk about why it hurt so bad that she wanted to die. He asked her if there was anyone she would consider talking to. Since I knew her, she asked for me. Sarah and I spent the next several hours together. She told me that she hated all guys. Her father had deserted her when she was eight years old. And now this stepfather, who had been a nice man, was sexually assaulting her. The pain went so deep that Sarah had lost all hope.

Together we sought help. We reported this tragedy first to the psychiatrist and then to a social worker, who spoke to the mother and stepfather. The stepfather eventually ended up in prison. Sarah went through extensive counseling, which helped her put her life together. Eventually she could see that she had been the victim of an extremely sick man. The counseling process gave her a reason to live—and a hope that life could be different.

Today, she isn't blaming herself. She still feels a tinge of pain when she thinks about the experience, but she has learned to move on. Not only does Sarah have two lovely children, but she and her husband also run a camp for battered and abused kids. She hung on to hope, and she would tell you it was the right thing to do.

God Cares; He Really Does

Most people who have experienced any kind of sexual abuse struggle in their relationship with God. Under the circumstances, I can understand why it might feel difficult to believe that God really does love them. It's easy to blame God and be angry instead of allowing Him to bring comfort. But God wants to walk with us through hurt and pain.

In the New Testament, John writes about how Jesus heard about the death of his friend Lazarus. When he saw the family grieving, "Jesus wept" (John 11:35). Jesus weeps for you when you have been hurt too.

Jesus knows a lot about suffering. After all, He suffered a painful death on the cross, just to make it possible for us to spend an eternity with God in heaven. I believe that Jesus would still have suffered on the cross if you were the only person in the world who needed Him.

If God loves you enough to allow His only Son to die for you, then I believe He cares deeply for you and your pain. And even though you can't always control the circumstances in your life, you can control your response to them. And that makes all the difference in the world.

If you have experienced sexual abuse, you don't have to continue to live in pain that is happening to you over and over as you re-live those experiences. You can take things into your own hands by talking to an adult you trust and getting help that leads to healing. It wasn't your choice to be abused, but healing *is* your choice. With God's help, you *can* overcome your pain. The decision to move toward help and healing is not always easy, but it is always the best.

Here's the question you have to answer: Who and where do you want to be in ten years?

The decisions you make today will affect you for the rest of your life. Choose health and healing; and remember, even through your darkest times, you are never alone. God, who created you and loves you, is near.

What Is Sexual Abuse?

The following information about sexual abuse is something I share when I'm speaking to students about this important but horrible subject.[1]

Nobody has the right to touch your body in a sexual way without your permission, regardless of how much he or she loves you, how much money they have spent on you, or for any other reason.

Any time a touch makes you feel uncomfortable, you have the right to say no. You never *owe* another person the right to touch you. Trust your gut feelings. Pressuring, manipulating, or abusing another person is never acceptable in any relationship.

If someone touches you in a way you don't like, tell that person to stop and get away. Then talk about it with an adult you trust.

If an adult or older teenager has touched you in the past, it is *not your fault*. It is *always* the abuser's responsibility.

It is *especially important* that you get counseling for sexual abuse *now,* to prevent problems as you grow older. If you have never talked with a counselor, reach out for help immediately.

Sexual assault involves instances where a person, whether male or female, is deceived, pressured, enticed, intimidated, controlled, or compelled to engage in sexual acts without their consent.

Sexual abuse can be defined as

- Showing children pornographic materials
- Taking nude pictures
- An adult exposing themselves to a child or asking the child to expose himself or herself
- Touching private areas of the body
- Intimate kissing
- Genital contact
- Sexual intercourse
- Rape

Sexual assault includes incest, molestation, rape, and date rape.

Incest is sexual activity between any relatives. Usually, this activity is started by a father or stepfather, grandfather, uncle, cousin, or brother. Occasionally a mother, grandmother, or aunt will start it.

Molestation is sexual activity with someone outside the person's family. Eighty percent of molestations are by someone the victim knows and trusts: a family friend, the mother's boyfriend, a neighbor, a teacher, a coach, a doctor or dentist, a pastor or priest, a youth leader, a camp counselor, or a baby-sitter. Only 20 percent of molestations are done by strangers.[2]

Rape is forced penetration (by penis or any object) of the vagina, mouth, or anus against the will of the victim.

Acquaintance rape or *"date rape"* is rape by someone you know or are dating. Date rapists generally use just enough force to gain compliance. A man may use his physical power to have intercourse or take advantage of a situation by using force, pressure, deception, trickery, or teen vulnerability. The date rapist is not a weird, easily identifiable person. He is just like anyone else—except that he uses force to get his way. About 75 percent of teen rapes are acquaintance or date rapes.[3]

What to Do If You Are Raped

If you are raped:

1. Get to a safe place.
2. *Do not* bathe, wash your private parts, or change clothes.
3. Call a rape crisis hotline. (The number for the National Sexual Assault Hotline is 1-800-656-4673.)
4. Go to the hospital emergency room. Have a friend or family member go with you to the hospital and take a change of clothes if possible. Do this as soon as possible to
   - Preserve the evidence
   - Determine the extent and nature of physical injury and receive treatment
   - Test for STDs and pregnancy

Reasons for Reporting the Rape

Reporting the crime to the police is a decision that only you can make. However, making a police report will help you. Reporting the assault is a way of regaining your own sense of personal power and control, because it lets you to do something concrete about the crime committed against you. Reporting the crime also helps ensure that you receive the best assistance available.

Making a police report will also help prevent other people from being raped. Reporting and prosecuting the person who raped you are essential to prevent rape. Most rapists have raped more than one person. If the rape is not reported, the rapist cannot be caught.

I know this is a hard chapter to read. But I hope that as you read it, you can also see there is hope. If you have ever been sexually abused in any way, you can get help. Sure, it will be difficult to talk with someone about it, but there is so much good that can come from it. When you open up about your story of the abuse you've experienced, you are giving the gift of healing to your life and to your future.

If you have never experienced the trauma of abuse, then reading this chapter can help you take the necessary precautions to help keep from being violated. At one time I hesitated to include this chapter in this book. After all, so much of making a commitment toward sexual integrity is a decision you make. And sexual abuse is not about a decision you make. Just know that if any of this chapter describes your life in any way, there is help and there is hope. Do the courageous thing and seek help. You will not regret it.

DISCUSSION STARTERS

Think about your answers to the questions below and talk about them with an adult you trust.

1. Why do you think it might be important to include a chapter on sexual abuse in a book on the Integrity Code?
2. Why do you think sexual abuse is so much more common in our culture today than when your parents were kids?
3. What are practical ways a person can lower their risk of sexual abuse?
4. What advice would you give to a friend who has experienced the devastation of sexual abuse?

NOTES

Note to Parents and Student Ministry Leaders

1. Madeleine L'Engle, *Walking on Water: Reflections on Faith and Art* (New York: Convergent Books, 2001).

Chapter 1 Awkward!

1. If you don't know who Big Bird is, he is from a cartoon called *Sesame Street*, and you can look at his photo if you Google it.

Chapter 2 Amazing!

1. Yuval Noah Harari, *Sapiens: A Brief History of Humankind* (Oxford, United Kingdom: Signal Books, 2014), 438.

Chapter 4 The Foundation

1. I have changed their names for privacy.

Chapter 5 Culture, Gender, and Authority

1. I'm deeply grateful to my pastor, Jeff Maguire, for unknowingly helping me with this chapter from an amazing sermon series he gave in the summer of 2023 called "Being Human." Harbor Point Church, San Juan Capistrano, CA.

2. John Mark Comer, *Live No Lies: Recognize and Resist the Three Enemies that Sabotage Your Peace* (Colorado Springs, CO: WaterBrook, 2021), 118.

3. Jackie Hill Perry, *Gay Girl, Good God: The Story of Who I Was, and Who God Has Always Been* (Nashville, TN: B&H, 2018).

4. The word *sin* means to "miss the mark." The "mark" in this case is living in God's will.

5. National Health Society, "Gender Dysphoria," NHS 111 Wales, last updated December 15, 2022, https://111.wales.nhs.uk/genderdysphoria.

6. Jeff Maguire, "The Sacred Self," message given on June 11, 2023, at Harbor Point Church, San Juan Capistrano, CA.

7. Dr. Preston Sprinkle is one of my favorite authors and leaders on a compassionate approach to gender while staying firm on the historical Christian biblical approach. You can find excellent resources by him at CenterForFaith.com.

Chapter 6 Changes in Your Body

1. This is obviously an oversimplification of the process. For a more in-depth look, I recommend that your parents or a trusted adult find a book, website, or pamphlet that solely focuses on this process.

Chapter 7 The Battle for Your Mind

1. Jannik Lindner, "Pornography Industry Statistics," Gitnux Market Data Report, last updated January 9, 2024, https://gitnux.org/pornography-industry-statistics.

2. Michael B. Robb and Supreet Mann, "Teens and Pornography," Common Sense Media, last updated January 5, 2024, https://www.commonsensemedia.org/sites/default/files/research/report/2022-teens-and-pornography-final-web.pdf

3. Over the past seven decades, rock and roll has evolved in many directions. Numerous styles of music—from soul to hip-hop, from heavy metal to punk, from progressive rock to electronic and even pop music—have fallen under the rock and roll umbrella.

Chapter 8 The Dangers of Pornography

1. www.CovenantEyes.com is a great resource to help you with resources, accountability, and counseling referrals.

Chapter 11 Flirting, Modesty, and How Far Is Too Far?

1. Hayley DiMarco, *Sexy Girls, How Hot Is Too Hot?* (Grand Rapids, MI: Revell, 2006), 105.

2. Pam Stenzel, *Sex Has a Price Tag: Discussions about Sexuality, Spirituality, and Self-Respect* (Grand Rapids, MI: Zondervan, 2003).

Chapter 12 Sexual Abuse

1. Jim Burns, "Sexual Abuse," HomeWord, May 7, 2018, https://homeword.com/jims-blog/sexual-abuse/.

2. Our Turn, "The Unspoken Subject," Turning Points Network, April 3, 2023, https://turningpointsnetwork.org/news/the-unspoken-subject -sexual-abuse/.

3. State of California Department of Justice, "Myths and Facts about Sexual Assault," California Megan's Law, accessed February 8, 2024, https://www.meganslaw.ca.gov/mobile/Education_MythsAndFacts.aspx.